Ke Garne?

Ke Garne?

Sustainable Christian Community Development in the Himalayas

With accompanying Bible Study Guide

Health Environmental and Learning Program

Lani Kay Ackerman, MD, FAAFP

authorHOUSE®

AuthorHouse™ LLC
1663 Liberty Drive
Bloomington, IN 47403
www.authorhouse.com
Phone: 1-800-839-8640

Photography (including cover) by Tim Ackerman

Published by AuthorHouse 04/08/2014

ISBN: 978-1-4918-4221-8 (sc)
ISBN: 978-1-4918-4222-5 (hc)
ISBN: 978-1-4918-4223-2 (e)

Library of Congress Control Number: 2013922699

Table of Contents

Foreword

Ke garne is a commonly used phrase in Nepal that literally means, "What to do?" It implies, in a fatalistic sense, that really there is nothing that can be done. This is the general attitude among many who live in the Himalayas as they look at what they perceive to be unchangeable events in life. Thankfully, the point of this book is that something *can* be accomplished, because mankind is *not* in an endless cycle of birth and rebirth. If development is based in Christian outreach and the principles of loving God first and loving our neighbor secondly, there is much that can be done for His glory.

Jesus looked at them and said, 'With man this is impossible, but with God all things are possible.' Matthew 19:26

During the courtship phase of our relationship, the one thing that most impressed me about my wife was the way she lived out God's Word. This habit in her relationship with the Lord helped set the basis for acting out the Great Commission in our lives.

But whoever looks intently into the perfect law that gives freedom, and continues in it—not forgetting what they have heard, but doing it—they will be blessed in what they do. James 1:25

In the 1990s, my wife and I experienced a paradigm shift in the way we approached and implemented our Gospel outreach to a small portion of the world virtually unreached with Christ. Instead of focusing on what we ourselves could do, we recognized the importance of educating and training those nationals through whom and with whom we were trying to accomplish sustainable Christian community development. The end result, we envisioned, should be that our own services would eventually not be needed.

As you read our story, leave time for contemplation. Ask some basic questions before planning a mission outreach: Is this the wisest use of the Lord's resources? How does the Lord want us to most effectively accomplish reaching the unreached world? Are we reaching a lost world through our current methods? Is the answer more short-term mission trips? Should we build more houses for the less fortunate or just give food to the poor? Why are we doing what we are doing? Could we be hurting others by our well-meaning efforts? We need to answer these questions with irrevocable scripture or guidance from the Lord, not just because "everybody else is doing it." I think you will find this book will help you to ask the right questions.

The Apostle Paul gives us wise advice:

> *Our hope is that, as your faith continues to grow, our sphere of activity among you will greatly expand, so that we can preach the gospel in the regions beyond you. For we do not want to boast about work already done in someone else's territory. But, 'Let the one who boasts boast in the Lord.'*
> 2 Corinthians 10:16-17

May God bless your pursuit and technique of taking the Gospel to a lost world and making disciples of all the nations.

Tim Ackerman, BS, MS Vertebrate Ecology

Preface

Therefore go and make disciples of all nations, baptizing them in the name of the Father and of the Son and of the Holy Spirit, and teaching them to obey everything I have commanded you . . . Matthew 28:19-20

The parting words of Jesus in what is known as The Great Commission comprise the biblical mandate for missions. The Western church, however, cannot fulfill Christ's mandate to go to all nations, when physically, culturally, and even geographically, we cannot reach the most needy. The 10-40 window[1] is the north-south latitude of the world enveloping the greatest poverty, largest population, and least exposure to the gospel. This geographical area continues to be the focus of only minimal resources of the Christian church, despite 20 years of emphasis and education by mission experts. Churches, development agencies, and missions continue to fund and send out workers to the easiest, most accessible and comfortable locations, even where there are established indigenous churches and national leadership. To reach these unreached areas as the hands and feet of Christ, with His love, we must look to the two greatest commandments that our Lord gave:

'Love the Lord your God with all your heart and with all your soul and with all your mind.' This is the first and greatest commandment. And the second is like it: 'Love your neighbor as yourself.' Matthew 22:37-39

---

[1]   For photo and definition refer to http://www.joshuaproject.net/10-40-window.php

Christian community development is a spiritual movement that develops communities not only in the physical sense, but also in the spiritual sense, so that believers might first love God, and secondly, love their neighbors as themselves. This book is not a missionary autobiography, but a story of how God has worked through a family to create a Christian community development program that has become a grassroots movement throughout parts of the Himalayas. For the purpose of clarity, the book is divided into two parts. Part One describes the personal aspects and vision of our family's journey that directly relate to how Health Environmental and Learning Program (H.E.L.P.) developed, while Part Two unfolds the process through which the movement developed, examining the transition to national-centered leadership. Because parts of this story took place (and continue to unfold) in areas sensitive to both Christian and development efforts, I have avoided naming specific places and have used alternative names, rather than names of some individuals, for their protection. The term "national" may also be replaced with "indigenous" and refers to a person born in and from that country, in contrast to missionaries or development workers from another country.

The Himalayas, a spectacularly beautiful mountain range to the north of the Indian subcontinent in Asia, span across Pakistan, China, Bhutan, Nepal, and India, in the center of the 10-40 window. As a whole, it is vastly undeveloped, with many people living as they have for thousands of years. The gospel has only recently reached many ethnic groups within this region, and many have still not heard of Christ. The terrain itself has been a barrier to outside visitors, ranging from the height of Mount Everest to the terai (lowlands) of Nepal. Health and development indices vary dramatically depending on access to roads, locality, and effects of civil conflict, but are among some of the most dismal in the world. It is here that our family has had the privilege to be the hands and feet of Christ, teaching others while learning how to love the Lord first and love our neighbor as ourselves.

This book is written for ambassadors of Christ who desire a wholistic, compassionate, sustainable, and financially viable means to minister to the physical and spiritual needs of the poor. Followers of Jesus must want no glory for themselves or their sending agency, but must want *God* to receive glory. We have found Christian community development to be the most Biblical means of carrying the gospel to the unreached. It empowers indigenous Christian leaders to establish their own, self-sufficient churches as well as to develop and improve the health and livelihood of their own people. It is a sustainable means to bring true, wholistic development (that is, development that encompasses the body, soul, and spirit) *through* the love of Christ.

Acknowledgements

I would like to acknowledge our wonderful friends, family, financial supporters, and prayer partners—especially our Health Environmental and Learning Program (H.E.L.P.) advisory board members. Most importantly, we must thank our Nepali brothers and sisters who essentially are H.E.L.P. in action. Their dedication to Christ and their own people is the reason for the transformation of lives and communities. Special thanks to my supportive husband and our four amazing children, all of whom helped with editing and writing various parts of this adventure, as well as for their understanding when I neglected them, working late into the night to complete this book.

Dedication

This book is dedicated to the memory of LeNelle Slack Douglas, my mother, who is with the Lord Jesus. Without her prayers, encouragement, and hard work in the early years of Health Environmental and Learning Program (H.E.L.P.), the miracles recorded in this book could never have happened.

Lani Ackerman, MD

Book One

Chapter 1

Those Who Have Never Heard

Divine Leading

"Though I'm Buddhist, I've read and studied about the gods of the Hindus and Muslims as well as other religions," commented Dorji, "but I think Christianity is the *true* way to God."

My husband, Tim, and I exchanged shocked glances at this comment. Was this really an answer to our prayers? It was 1990, and we had been invited by the government of a small, isolated kingdom in the Himalayas to evaluate their hospitals and propose a project for educating newly graduated doctors who had no opportunity for internship, residency, or further continuing education. For me, as a young family physician and professor, and for Tim, a Colorado environmentalist and wildlife biologist, it was Shangri-La.[2]

Nearly every minute of our three-week approved visit was under close supervision, but finally we had an afternoon to relax without a representative from the department of health. While hiking a trail to admire the architecture of the Buddhist monasteries and the spectacular beauty of the mountains, we met Dorji. We had just finished listening to a cassette tape about evangelizing the world, and we had intensely prayed that the Lord would provide us with an opportunity to share the salvation message with someone in this

---

[2] *Shangri-La* represents a particular area in the Himalayas still closed to the gospel, where persecution is intense. Because of the sensitive nature of both gospel and development work, this term is used to describe the area to protect those serving Christ there today.

country of less than 40 known Christians of the predominant people group.[3] Many of the educated in the area spoke English. Dorji, a high school student beginning nursing studies, noticed us (not surprising in a country where few foreigners lived at that time) and offered to accompany us up the steep mountain to the monastery where he would be leading Buddhist prayers. While most of the people in this nation had never even heard the name of Christ, this young man had prayed for a chance to meet the God he did not know.

"Why do you say that Christianity might be the truth, and what do you know of Christianity?" Tim asked.

Dorji told us of his search for salvation and truth. He had worshiped Buddha and many idols. As a Tibetan Buddhist, he believed salvation—that is, escaping from the wheel of life and continual reincarnation—came through meditation and the eight-fold path of suffering taught by Gautama Buddha. Over the course of that day we became Dorji's friends and spiritual parents. His open heart received the message that the death and resurrection of Jesus Christ pays for our sins and breaks the wheel of life.[4] At his first exposure to the gospel, he trusted Christ as his Savior and renounced idolatry. Through prayer and the work of the Holy Spirit, we were ready for the divine appointment that God had prepared prior to our arrival. No Bible had yet been translated into his language, but he could read and write in English. We left him the only Bible we had brought—a large study

---

[3]   People group refers to a distinctive ethnic group with its own language and culture or "ethnos."

[4]   The wheel of life (*bhavacakra*) is a symbolic representation of *saṃsara* (cyclic existence) central to Tibetan Buddhism. Through his sacrifice, Christ breaks the cycle of reincarnation and frees the believer to enter communion with God and receive eternal life.

Bible—and promised to ask the Lord for an opportunity to return and disciple him.

Called to Missions

When we met Dorji, we had been married less than a year. I was in both clinical and academic medicine, teaching residents at a family medicine residency program in Fort Worth, Texas. Tim worked in the environmental department of the US Army Corps of Engineers. After committing to Christ to be a missionary doctor at age seven, I finished medical school at twenty-two, had completed a three-year family medicine residency, and was at a Southwestern Baptist Theological Seminary studying missions and theology when we met. My calling was to take the gospel to those who had never heard through medicine, and the imminence of Christ's return drove me to embark into missionary medicine to share Christ as soon as possible. I had served in a traditional mission hospital setting in Ghana during residency, as well as in a mission hospital in the Amazon jungle in Ecuador.

Tim grew up Catholic and came to Christ personally in a charismatic Protestant church while serving in the US Army. Though he knew little about missions or international development, he loved mountain climbing, cross-country skiing, and cycling. He had spent most of his free time in athletic activities and environmental studies, such as tracking moose and wolves. After we met, he served in a short-term international experience with an agriculture mission agency, but God had been preparing him in the years before by giving him the rough adventure spirit that enabled us to survive physically daunting challenges in our future. It took God's sense of humor to bring together two people with such different backgrounds and talents, but it was through this balance, and our team approach, that He used (and continues to use) our skills.

Our meeting with Dorji in Shangri-La was a miracle in itself. Shortly after we were married, Tim and I began calling and sending requests to various mission boards in search of an opportunity that would use our professional skills for the purpose of sharing the gospel in a country with Tibetan Buddhist people groups, and which was closed[5] to traditional missions. I had studied the writings of the Dalai Lama and beliefs of Tibetan Buddhists while in seminary, and God had made it clear to me that He wanted us to work among people groups following this religion. We were convinced that we should be at least partial "tentmakers"[6] just like the apostle Paul, the greatest missionary example in the Bible. Because of this, we searched for opportunities where we would receive a small salary for our work, which we could subsidize with funds that we had been saving for this very calling. After innumerable letters and phone calls, we contacted an international mission agency that worked in the exact country to which we felt God calling us. The telephone conversation went something like this:

"I am a family physician on faculty in a residency program, my husband is an environmentalist, and we feel called to live and work among the Tibetan Buddhists living in the Himalayas, particularly in Shangri-La."

"We have never had a request like that, and the area is now closed, not requesting any volunteers," explained the administrator.

---

[5]   *Closed* is used to describe countries which typically have an underground church and require all foreigners to have a professional job in order to hold a work visa; they do not allow open evangelism and followers of Christ suffer great persecution.

[6]   *Tentmaker* refers to the fact that the Apostle Paul met his personal needs through the trade of making tents, enabling him to be a self-sufficient missionary. This is in contrast to the common practice of missionaries receiving a salary through the sending agency or church, or even raising all their expenses through supporters.

The very next day she returned our call and explained, with excitement in her voice, "I have just received a request for a family physician with academic qualifications to start a residency (post-graduate) program among the Tibetan Buddhist people of the Himalayas in Shangri-La; there is also a school training the country's leaders in environmental sciences which needs a teacher. This has never happened before, but we must do all we can to get you into this position." Clearly, this direction was the hand of God.

A few months later, the director of health in Shangri-La granted us a one-month visa so that I could visit and prepare a report on the condition of medical education in the country, as well as write my recommendations for a post-graduate training program for their doctors. Depending on this proposal, we might, or might not, be offered a more permanent position. During the long waiting period, we had already promised to provide two months of relief to overworked doctors at a mission hospital in Bangladesh. After much prayer, we decided to combine the relief work with the fact-finding tour of Shangri-La.

First, we spent two months in the hill tracts of Bangladesh in a desperately poor, underserved area, prayerfully considering it as a possibility for long-term work. While I examined and treated patients from dawn to dusk, Tim assisted in environmental work, evangelism, and video production for the hospital. Though our time was short, the experiences of examining hundreds of patients suffering from end-stage preventable diseases deeply influenced my views on the hopelessness of curative care and necessity of preventive health care in the developing world. From there, we flew to Shangri-La and traveled for a month through the country, gleaning information on the condition of health care and medical education of doctors. It was during this time that we met Dorji.

We returned to our jobs to await the government's decision on whether my proposal for the internship would be accepted. About six months after the visit, just when we were beginning to wonder if God would open a door for us to go, we arrived home and found our mailbox missing. It had been vandalized! Worried that there could have been a letter from the government, we prayed about the missing mail. The following morning, someone scattered mail covered with tire tracks across our front yard. In that mail was a letter from the ministry of health, offering a two-year visa and job assignment in Shangri-La. God had opened the door for us to return, fulfilling our promise to Dorji!

We were able to serve as professionals for two amazing years, utilizing our skills, sharing our lives, teaching the gospel, and discipling through friendships in the spectacular land of Shangri-La. (Fig 1.1-1.6) We had never before experienced the depth of spiritual darkness or the physical and mental oppression one senses when people worship demonic spirits. In spite of hardships, we grew to love the people whose country we shared. Both Tim and I developed deep and meaningful friendships. He spent hours playing and coaching basketball (and participated in a tournament in which his team defeated the king's team), while I enjoyed baking cookies with the queen's sister and cousins or inviting a hundred guests for Christmas goodies. Before and after work, our tiny apartment averaged thirty visitors a day, including many neighborhood children who came to hear Bible stories, or just to see a foreigner.

Initially, our greatest culture shock stemmed from simple annoyances. In this Buddhist society, stray dogs could not be killed (except during a rabies epidemic), so nighttime became a competition:

sleep versus noise from packs of howling dogs and chanting lamas[7] performing incantations. On one occasion, we arrived home to find our third-floor wood apartment surrounded by smoke. Relieved that it was not a fire, we were shocked to realize our downstairs neighbor was conducting a *puja*. [8] A notoriously picky eater from childhood, I determined to do my best at cultural adjustment and eat whatever the locals ate. The entire country had only one "western" store which sold poor quality cocoa powder and absolutely no chocolate candy, so meals consisted of rice, chilies, yak cheese, and lentils. Initially convinced by the condition of the local meat market to be a vegetarian, Tim later learned to decapitate chickens and patiently waited in line for the leanest piece of pork—an easy task since pork fat was a local favorite and the lean cuts were always the last to be purchased. Lemon tea was our preference over the more locally popular butter tea (made with rancid butter), but both were palatable when it was cold enough outside. Though daily life was difficult, the novelty of the culture and our commitment to demonstrating the love of Christ made these years a time when we built some of our deepest friendships.

An Impossible Task

Not long after unloading hundreds of books we had shipped for a medical library, I came to the realization that my official task to develop a program for the newly graduated medical doctors was likely impossible. Though the country's director of health approved my position, the few existing local physicians did not support me. I was forced to work in a system over which I had no control, sometimes

---

[7]   A spiritual leader and tantric teacher of Tibetan Buddhism in the monastery.

[8]   A religious ceremony that involves sacrifices or other activities to appease demonic spirits.

under the authority of arrogant, poorly trained doctors. Consequently, I soon realized I could either quit, or be flexible and assume a different role.

Rather than the leadership role I had enjoyed both during short-term international experiences and as a faculty and clinician in the United States, I found myself in a service-oriented role developing continuing medical education courses for the doctors in remote areas of the country, utilizing my expertise, and that of others, to provide up-to-date information. Since the specialty of family medicine was unknown, I filled whatever need the country's referral hospital had, depending on who was available. Most of the local physicians had little more than a medical diploma, and volunteers for a few months to a few years from countries all over Asia filled the "consultant" positions. These professionals varied greatly in their professional ability and degree of concern for the locals, presenting an interesting combination of care at the one tertiary care center of the nation. I saw patients with every imaginable condition and grew greatly in my understanding and knowledge of diseases common to the Himalayan people. I spent several months supervising rows of critically ill children or babies, followed by months handling complicated gynecologic affairs. When there were no experienced physicians in adult medicine, my role became supervising the nation's drug-resistant tuberculosis treatment while managing the most complicated internal medicine cases. During this time, I continued to make attempts to develop at least a rotating internship for new graduates, but the majority of these bright young men were not from the ethnicity of the ruling class. I soon began to realize that the government had begun a program of ethnic cleansing, and young doctors of the wrong ethnicity were daily "disappearing" to a refugee camp or to places unknown.

Tim's teaching position was more collegial, but both of us experienced roles unlike that of a traditional missionary or international development worker. As we desired to live lives of service to Christ, sharing our faith in Him as we developed friendships, these opportunities were priceless. During my days in the clinic and hospital, Tim taught environmental science courses and drank tea while talking about politics, religion, or life. One day, while Tim was enjoying a cup of tea and conversation with a prominent young man, Sonam, he leaned over and confided to Tim, "you're not like the other foreigners; you really are my friend." Tim also enjoyed riding his mountain bike over 17,000-foot peaks and through yak herds, and playing basketball with his students and others. Most importantly, we learned how to minister and work together as a couple in a totally different culture with minimal support and rare letters from home.

In 1991, Shangri-La had strict laws forbidding outside radio, television, newspapers, or communication, and even legally dictated a dress code. As two of six Americans in the country, our open apartment attracted visitors of all types. Buddhist monks, beggars, and high-ranking officials found their way into our living room. Some stayed for an hour and talked politics. Others stayed for a week and stole small items they could find. We began to understand more of the struggles, culture, and religion of the people whom we loved. We were not there just to share the truth of the Gospel and teach them more in the areas of medicine and ecology, we were there to learn from them as well. We were working as professionals, as salt and light in a nation full of darkness and demonic spirits—not in a protected mission compound environment surrounded by like-minded laborers. While this was incredibly difficult, it taught us humility and a servant's heart that won the respect and friendship of our colleagues, allowing them to see Christ in us in a way that they otherwise could have never witnessed. We quietly taught the Bible to a small group of national believers, including Dorji, while building true friendships with those of other beliefs.

Through our friendships, we began to appreciate deep truths of the spiritual world, which we had never appreciated in the West. One friend, Pasang, had never heard of Christ but confided, "During a time of serious illness, when my family gave me up to death, I saw a man in white talking with a man in black. The man in white was kind, and He refused to let the man in black take me. I awoke, and I later realized the one who saved me from death was Christ."

John, from a neighboring country, was translating the Bible into his local language. He came to visit his daughter, who was our dear friend, and we learned how God miraculously revealed Himself to John while he was a lama in the Buddhist monastery. We also experienced the harsh realities of life when he and most of his family died from multidrug-resistant tuberculosis; only his daughter survived the disease.

The price believers paid in this part of the world was not limited to loss of family ties and finances; it often included prison, death, or spiritual attack. As we recognized the strong spiritual and cultural barriers to following Christ, we were faced with a sobering fact: the very few young believers were predominately of a different ethnicity than the ruling class, and they were illiterate, uneducated, and desperately poor. They were ill-equipped to share the good news of Christ with their own families, much less with other ethnic groups within their country. Their daily battles involved simple survival.

Sonam and Karma, a middle-class Buddhist couple, were but one example of the intense spiritual warfare faced by those interested in the gospel. Close national Christian friends came over one evening, seeking our help with Karma. She had recently delivered a baby, then three months old, and over the past weeks had refused to feed the baby. Sonam was desperate; formula was not available, and he was searching for another lactating mother to keep his baby alive. Our friends recognized this was more than just post-partum depression.[9] It was a spiritual attack. At the request of Sonam, who was searching to know the true God, we began praying for Karma. She began shrieking and crying out, demanding in another voice that we stop. When we started singing praises to Christ, it became clear that she was demon possessed, as she demanded, "Stop it, stop that singing." After hours of prayer with no change in her demeanor, we searched for any items that could be hindering God's work. We saw that Sonam wore a Buddhist image on his necklace.

"If you are going to follow Christ and protect your wife from demonic attacks, you must leave idols," pleaded Tim. Sonam ripped the chain off of his neck and threw the icon out the window.

Shortly after, Karma vomited and became quieter. It seemed the demonic spirits had left her, and Sonam thanked us. A few days later, however, her symptoms recurred. Desperate, and doubting the reality of Christ, they approached the Buddhist lamas for appeasement of the demons. Later she was hospitalized and treated with multiple drugs in an attempt to help her. To our knowledge, she never recovered.

My interaction with patients enabled me to witness some of the first dramatic miraculous healings I had seen in my career. I prayed over a dying young man with typhoid and saw him healed, but was later reported to the government and reprimanded. A young woman with advanced cervical cancer left Buddhism and followed Christ. I examined her and told the family to expect death soon. The local believers prayed—and she was completely healed. Our

---

[9] A condition after childbirth from a hormonal imbalance, resulting in depression.

experiences—the spiritual warfare, the personal growth, and the miraculous healings—could fill another book.

Because of the lack of obstetrical care, a blood bank, or adequate medical facilities (and at the insistence of our mission) we briefly left Shangri-La for the birth of our first child, Kristen. We returned when she was six weeks old. We were promised another two-year visa, and came with extra luggage that included unavailable toys, books, and items for her to enjoy. Buried in the baby items, beneath a few stuffed animals, we hid huge quantities of books and Bibles for the underground church, which still had no Bible in the local language. When we went to collect our boxes and bags, a guard at the airport stopped us.

"Please open your boxes and bags for inspection," he demanded.

Though we were followed, watched closely, and spied on, we had never had our bags searched or been treated less than cordially. Presumably, there had been a recent smuggling of gold into the country, prompting the crackdown, and as the guard was lifting the stuffed animals hiding the theological books and Bibles (and we were desperately praying), our neighbor and good friend, a supervisor at the airport, stepped up and admonished the officials for searching us. We were able to deliver all the desperately needed resources to the fledgling church.

Three months later, however, there was a knock at our door. "I told you to stop having Bible studies, because the lamas are angry," said one of our best friends, an educated, prominent Buddhist young man who loved us dearly.

"Get packed. I saw a letter go across my desk, and they are going to throw you out fast!" confided another close companion.

A friend who worked for the UN had just informed us that our newly acquired phone had been bugged and our house was watched around the clock. Thankfully, by God's grace, we had time to pack, say good-byes, and book a flight on the day for which our visas were abruptly terminated. Had our gracious friends not warned us, we would have had merely three days to get ready to leave. In years past, Christians working in that part of the world had suffered a much worse fate, death. But to us, it seemed the same: we were devastated!

We had quit our jobs, sold our belongings, given up our careers, and sacrificed all to come to minister here. We spent our own savings to cover many costs, including books and materials for the physician training program that I was supposed to be directing. It seemed that God had abandoned us, and that our years in Shangri-La were a loss. Exhausted, devastated, disillusioned, and financially broke, a spiritual draining and depression (which we had never felt before) took root.

Though we had intended to spend many more years in Shangri-La, we awakened to the fact that the most spiritually and physically needy parts of the world often have governments that do not welcome development from Christians, or on occasion, *any* outsiders. We also recognized that for first-generation believers of the fledgling church in closed countries, renouncing their family's religion could mean loss of their means of livelihood and all family ties. In addition, these new believers often could not read or write, even *if* they did have a Bible translation in their heart language, and were surrounded by a culture and tradition totally in opposition to the gospel. Dorji, in fact, did continue in his growth, and after graduation from nursing school, worked many years while being transferred from region to region as punishment for his continued preaching. As a result, God used him in planting more new churches and evangelizing even more people who had never previously heard the name of Christ. After suffering in prison on two occasions, due to the "crime" of sharing his faith in Christ, he lost his job and became a full-time evangelist, with his wife and other national believers working to support him. He continues to do so today.

After our two years in Shangri-La, God allowed us to see some spiritual and physical results, but the young church was still ill equipped. Most of the people living in rural areas were illiterate, suffering and dying from common infectious

> The abrupt termination of our visas shocked us, and awakened us to the reality that our first priority must always be to train local followers of Christ to survive economically and physically, as well as spiritually.

diseases without even basic knowledge of health or agriculture, and lacking in development in every way. Backsliding into idolatry was the rule rather than the exception, especially for those from the Tibetan Buddhist world. God planted ideas in our minds that later developed into a vision for sustainable Christian community development—but we were not quite ready yet.

Biblical Principles

1. *Those who have never heard the gospel need to hear before they can believe.*

   The father of missions, the Apostle Paul, wrote: "How can they believe in the one of whom they have not heard? And how can they hear without someone preaching to them? . . . How beautiful are the feet of those who bring good news!" Romans 10:14-15

   Though we had studied and experienced international missions, and we knew the burden God had given us to bring Christ to unreached people groups of the Himalayas, it is a sobering experience to talk to person after person who has never heard of Christ and has no idea who He is. While most mission resources in the West are directed to areas of the world that already have the gospel, Christ is calling believers of the 21ˢᵗ century beyond the traditional mission fields to focus on the area of the world with the most people, most poverty, and fewest followers of Christ.

2. *Traditional or even "tentmaker" missionaries must recognize that we may not be able to stay long-term in the parts of the world most needing both the gospel and our professional skills.*

We must effectively train nationals to carry on our work, following the example of the Apostle Paul. (Acts 18:1-3) Though we did have a handful of young followers of Christ who continued to grow after we left, we had not adequately equipped them in a wholistic way to meet their physical needs.

Chapter 2

Incarnational Missions

Laying Fresh Groundwork

Nearly five years had passed since we left the Tibetan Buddhist world, and we were older, somewhat wiser, and certainly more numerous. When we left Shangri-La, our daughter Kristen was six months old. In addition to spiritual struggles, we witnessed the painful division of a country involved in an ethnic cleansing, and other human rights abuses. It took nearly two years for us to recover physically and spiritually from the intense ministry we had led. God had, in His wisdom, rescued us from complete burnout.

Shortly after our untimely return to the US, we were both able to resume our previous employment and find a place to live. I developed an international global health tract at the family medicine residency program where I taught, published more in the medical literature, and started a refugee clinic; Tim grew professionally in his career in wetlands management and environmental work. Our family, which soon grew by two more children, worked together to resettle refugees from all over the world. When we were not helping new friends from Sudan, Somalia, Kurdistan, or Bosnia, we hosted international students and developed relations with young people from India, China, and Thailand. Even our toddlers chose toys to share with their international friends. Tim also studied anthropology and cultural courses at Summer Institute of Linguistics (Wycliffe Bible translators), while I explored an ethnomusicology course on the side.

These years were foundational for developing a Biblical view of missions, and we continued to read, study, and understand other cultures as God gave us a vision for a new type of mission organization. We met colleagues working in Bible translation and study of minority languages in the Himalayas, and we continued friendships with some we had met previously. We also led a home fellowship group and assisted our growing church in developing a missions and international outreach program, while supporting ourselves through our own income.

We prayed and asked, "Lord, if you want us back in the Himalayas, provide a way and the means." The door to Shangri-La was sealed shut, but we applied to a variety of organizations that placed volunteer Christian professionals in developing countries, requesting a position in another Himalayan country with many Tibetan Buddhists. A position opened for Tim to be the environmental coordinator of a large hydropower project located in a remote rural area of Nepal. We naively thought I could practice medicine as time allowed, while homeschooling our three children. Again, our official capacity would be working as professionals in our fields.

> **We intended to go back to the neediest areas of the world, but this time with the intent to *work ourselves out of a job* and turn leadership over to national Christians, *empowering them* to develop their own nation and reach their own people, as soon as they were fully trained.**

At that time, Nepal was still a Hindu kingdom strongly opposed and to proselytism.[10] We did not receive even a small salary, as we had previously, but were funded through a combination of our own savings and donations from churches and generous individuals. Our jobs and visas were administered through a nominally Christian umbrella organization, which was authorized by the Nepali government to oversee many international mission organizations.

Once we received news about the job offer for Tim, we began praying for a means to incorporate the mission principles God was teaching us, as well as our vision for sustainable Christian community development. In addition, we had to raise significant financial support to cover administrative costs of the national mission organization that seconded us to the umbrella organization that, in turn, seconded us to two more organizations and finally to the hydropower project! We realized that to minimize administrative costs and funnel all of God's funds directly to His work on the mission field, as well as to alleviate miscommunication and confusion, starting a Christian development mission based in the United States (with plans to nationalize) would be the most efficient and effective option. With prayer and fasting we asked the Lord to help us outline a plan of action for what *He* wanted us to develop. My mother, who had a burden for reaching the unreached for Christ as well as experience in setting up tax-exempt organizations, helped us fill out the papers for submission to the IRS as a tax-exempt, 501 (c) (3) non-profit organization. Health

---

[10]   *Proselytism* refers to trying to convince others to change their faith, particularly through any forcible means—a practice with which we totally disagree. It can, however, be interpreted to mean *any* activity which encourages an individual to choose a religion different from his or her family or previous religion.

Environmental and Learning Program (H.E.L.P.)—that name fit the vision God was giving us—was born on paper.

Though *health* was the first word in the name, our experiences and study proved to us that basic literacy was foundational to health, church planting, and even economic development. Years before, I had used pictures to illustrate concepts to women caring for their malnourished babies in the bush of Ghana, Africa. Embedded in my mind was a young woman who, upon seeing a picture of a cow in the book declared, "Doctor, that is not a cow, *that* is a cow," while pointing to the animal in the field. I realized then, and recognized more during my studies in public health, that true illiteracy—even pictorial illiteracy—must be addressed and cured to have lasting development of any kind. Both Tim and I had witnessed the huge gap between the few educated, and the masses of illiterate villagers who did not even understand the link between filth and disease.

The tiny first-generation church with whom we had worked in Shangri-La was plagued with simple, preventable diseases that stemmed not just from lack of medical facilities, but also from lack of basic health education. Tim had seen the ravages of deforestation and landslides affecting Nepal and India, and he included a focus on addressing deforestation and sanitation. I had treated thousands of patients for simple diseases preventable by clean water and a safe cooking stove (instead of an open fire). Many friends and patients died from infectious diseases related to poor living conditions, lack of income, and malnutrition. All of these experiences were instrumental in directing the formation and written documentation for H.E.L.P.

A Vision for National Leadership and Sustainability

From the inception of our vision we planned to place committed, vibrant locals in charge of all programs, and to focus on prevention and a proactive approach rather than curative and relief efforts. Numerous experiences combined to shift our thinking away from traditional missionary models and standard development methods. In Ecuador, I had the privilege of working alongside dedicated missionaries who followed the martyrs Jim Elliot and Nate Saint.[11] I recognized the effects of prolonged missionary contact, however, especially the difficulty in developing the abilities of nationals when missionaries stay in the field for many years. In Bangladesh, I witnessed the legacy and selfless service of Dr. Viggo Olson[12] and others, but felt the futility of treating the masses suffering from preventable illness. In other mission hospitals, we saw inappropriate dependence on foreigners for expertise and their continued monopoly of high-level positions. The abrupt termination of our visas in Shangri-La awakened us to the reality that even as professionals, our visas and positions could be terminated without notice, which necessitated a program that would be sustainable with local resources and leaders.

First, we believed, H.E.L.P. must *empower nationals*—that is, indigenous people—to develop their own country. It must be a ministry in which first-generation believers are equipped to care for

---

[11] Jim Elliot, Nate Saint, and their team were young missionaries who were martyred in 1958 by the stone-age tribe of Auca Indians in Ecuador. Nate's sister, Rachel, and Jim's wife, Elisabeth, later returned to take the gospel to these people, who turned to Christ. The incredible story is recounted in *Jungle Pilot* by Russell T. Hitt (Discovery House Publishers, 1959) and *Through Gates of Splendor*, by Elisabeth Elliot (Tyndale Momentum, 1981).

[12] Dr. Olson, an atheist turned Christian surgeon, served the people of East Pakistan during their civil war through the birth of Bangladesh and established Memorial Christian Hospital. His testimony to God's greatness and autobiography is *Daktar: Diplomat of Bangladesh,* by Viggo Olson (Kregel Publications, 1996).

and demonstrate the love of Christ to their own and then, in turn, demonstrate that love to their neighbors.

"Love the Lord your God with all your heart and with all your soul and with all your strength. Love your neighbor as yourself."
Deuteronomy 6:5, Matthew 19:19

Secondly, we hoped to become "tentmakers" like the Apostle Paul. We planned to train others and leave leadership in the hands of those locals, allowing us to support ourselves financially, give of our own resources, and direct funds as needed for the national staff and programs.

In an almost prophetic manner, directed by the Holy Spirit, we wrote down these ideas of a sustainable Christian community development program: literacy, income generation, agriculture, animal husbandry, sanitation, environmental improvement. Neither of us had ever seen, read about, or heard of such a program. In October 1997, we submitted our non-profit application to the IRS and prayed with our partners and supporters that God would allow us to begin the mission organization. When we reflect back on that time now, we are amazed at how God gave us ideas and placed us in positions and with people whom He used to develop this community-based organization that is now dramatically impacting the Himalayan region.

> We had seen the need and witnessed some of the components we wanted to include, in other ministries, but exactly how each "facet" would interrelate was a concept we only hoped *could* develop. In short, H.E.L.P. was a divine experiment.

It took one and a half years for approval as a non-profit organization. In order to officially reside in-country and have a work visa, we needed to work with the umbrella mission through which we had found Tim's environmental position. After resigning our jobs in Texas, we suddenly received news that, due to another government change, our visa to Nepal had been denied. Though we did not understand God's plan, we prayed and asked for His direction. Within a week, our house sold and I was offered a faculty position at a residency program in the town where my parents were living.

We had already survived one experience of selling all and going to the field, only to be kicked out unceremoniously and to return unexpectedly with a child, no money, and no home. This new unforeseen blessing provided us an opportunity to purchase a home as a base and to establish another home church. Though our departure was delayed seven months, this visa change proved our salvation when this south Texas town became the U. S. roots for our children. In addition, many of our new church friends became prayer warriors and financial supporters of Health Environmental and Learning Program (H.E.L.P.).

Return to the Himalayas

In January 1998, we stepped off a plane into the smog-saturated Kathmandu valley. Kristen (age five), Aaron (age three), and Austin (age one), were shivering with cold and anticipation. Their coat pockets were stuffed with all imaginable snacks and toys that had to provide entertainment during the arduous three-day journey. Friends we had met during a brief stay in Kathmandu in 1991 welcomed us at the airport and escorted us to the living quarters assigned for our three-month language study. The Nepali "umbrella" mission organization required we live in their guest house and pay exorbitant fees to support the organization; however, there was no regular electricity, no wood stoves for heat, layers of thick pollution, and deep spiritual oppression. For several months we suffered interminable illness and misery during which our family lived in a 15 × 15 foot unheated concrete room with minimal toilet facilities and rarely functional electricity.

The children, as well as Tim and I, suffered physically and spiritually. On one occasion, Aaron, in an attempt to find us, escaped from the daycare where he stayed during our language school, despite the watchful eye of his older sister and the staff. Thankfully, his blue eyes and white hair, as well as his small stature, attracted the attention of the Nepalese, who recognized he had escaped and rescued him before he was hit by a car on the busy streets of the capital. Both boys developed asthma from the thick pollution and, despite my best efforts, drove me to desperation to find a way to leave the city. The mission organization finally conceded to allow us to house-sit for a furloughing family in a cleaner part of Kathmandu, but noted in our files that we were "difficult and lacking in submission to their authority."

After three months of continued illness and inadequate language study, we received approval to move to the village of our official assignment. We later found out that onsite personnel had strongly recommended against new expatriate (foreign) families moving to this location due to the difficult physical and spiritual situation at the project, dangerous political conditions, and impossible job expectations into which Tim would be thrust. The wife of the previous expatriate project director had become psychotic and attempted to murder her house help; several of the other families had been removed due to physical and mental health issues. This challenging setting provided God's next training ground to prepare our family to lead a mission organization with a unique approach.

Initially, our new home fit my ideal—incarnational missions! After the nightmare of nearly losing Aaron and Austin to asphyxiation from asthma attacks, it was a relief to be in a pollution-free environment—well, free from vehicle pollution, at least. There were other types of pollution, like wood smoke from kitchen fires, human feces littering the trails, rotting compost, and animal manure. Since my call to missions as a child, my vision of ministering was living in a mud hut with few amenities; living like the locals—no mission compounds! From our experience as short-termers at the mission compound in Bangladesh and my work in Ghana and Ecuador in the traditional setting of a mission hospital, we felt that though God had used these institutions to bring the gospel and healing to new areas, national believers could not sustain these large institutions. God was leading us to develop a different type of outreach. In addition, we felt that God had called us to be "with the people" so that we could have greater impact as Christian development workers.

On the day of arrival to the village, our new neighbors came out to meet us and (unbeknown to us) to examine our belongings. We immediately loved Hajur-Ama (grandmother), who as the mother of thirteen children was related to most of the village (Fig 2.2). She and her family became our practical cultural guides to life in a Nepali village, and they were instrumental in the future development of H.E.L.P., which was at that time more a vision than a reality.

Our house was quaint—a "modern" three-story mud home (total height of about 15 feet), complete with an indoor squat potty (standard Asian toilet), a faucet for running water in the kitchen (though often there was not water), and plastic covering the thatch roof that served as the ceiling (so shrews and mice that ran through the roof did not fall onto the kitchen table). The bottom floor had two windows that opened into Hajur-Ama's water buffalo wallow, facing the kitchen where her daughter-in-law, Devi, cooked using a traditional open fire. The top floor was only 4 feet tall, intended primarily for storing grain; however, it served as a wonderful play area for Kristen and could be accessed by a treacherous stairway that enticed newly mobile Austin. Within the first month, we were immersed in the culture; our language acquisition improved rapidly. (Fig 2.1, 2.3, 2.4)

The children loved the village. They could run in the fields between rice paddies and observe the neighbor's chickens, livestock, and smelly water buffalo. Although we had no plan for a house helper, our friends assured us that this would assist our transition to village life; in fact, we had inherited her as a helper and had no choice. Soon, between homeschooling and trying to clean a mud house, or "muddy house," as the boys called it after spilling water to run their toy cars through, I had to agree. Though I wanted my time to be focused on the children, the medical needs of the community were great.

Unsuccessful Attempts

Tim jumped into his job as environmental coordinator of the hydropower project and spent his days hiking up and down mountains, surveying community projects such as literacy, reforestation, and sanitation. (Fig 2.5) I began to examine and treat patients in an under-fives[13] clinic focusing on the malnutrition and health needs of young children, as well as examining pregnant women, delivering babies, and assisting as needed in the hydropower project clinic. Initially, there was no other doctor for hundreds of miles; later, a kind but inexperienced national doctor was hired by the hydropower project. Judy, a nurse practitioner whose family was the only other American family in the area, also volunteered in the clinic. She and her husband (working with Tim) also served as professionals through a denominational mission

---

[13]   *Under-fives* denotes children under age five who are at highest risk for malnutrition and death from infectious diseases.

board under the same umbrella organization; they and their children became some of our dearest friends and lifelong prayer partners.

A few days after arriving in our new village home, women started bringing their children with open, oozing sores to the door, asking for medicine to help. Armed with our public health knowledge, we purchased local soap and demonstrated proper bathing at the village tap. Water was a luxury carried from the mountains and streams until the hydropower project built a village tap to provide easier access. Unaccustomed to available water, the women did not realize the connection between washing and health. Within a short time, most of the children were "healed" of their skin ailments using this simple soap and water technique. Our first attempt at teaching hygiene was a roaring success!

Less than a week after arrival, a local nurse midwife from the project clinic rushed to our door, shouting: "There is a lady with a bad delivery, come quickly!"

I raced at top speed across the fields, praying God would help me. When I ran in the door, the outcome was obvious. The woman was lying on a bed with the umbilical cord visibly protruding. It was a cord prolapse, a condition in which the umbilical cord of the placenta delivers before the baby, cutting off the oxygen supply. Only in the best of circumstances, if a baby can be delivered within minutes of a cord prolapse, is there any hope of survival. I immediately delivered the baby and began resuscitation, but it was too late. I handed the exhausted lady her dead infant, and left thinking how different the outcome could have been, had the baby been delivered sooner.

On another occasion, I was roused in the middle of the night to attend to a neighbor who had just delivered. The mother-in-law (*sasura*) attending the delivery (as traditionally practiced), was by the patient, who was unconscious.

"What happened, I gasped," having run rapidly over uneven terrain with a flashlight in hand.

"She delivered the baby, but hasn't spoken since," replied her *sasura*. "But don't touch her . . ." she commented as I pulled on my gloves to quickly conduct an internal exam and do uterine massage after feeling her thready, barely palpable pulse.[14]

In rural Nepal, women have shorter life expectancy than men because of high maternal mortality. In many areas, less than two percent of women have any medical supervision during delivery, and only a fraction have access to medical or surgical facilities where a cesarean section can be performed in cases of obstructed labor or fetal distress.[15] After a few months of dealing with obstetrical cases in the villages, I realized that the information we had read about traditional birth assistants (TBAs) and village health workers was correct—in a country like this, educating more local women to understand women's health and pregnancy was the only hope for changing outcomes. Some large organizations reportedly had success in other parts of the country training TBAs, so perhaps I could, too. After all, I reasoned, I was an experienced doctor and professor, and I was fairly fluent in the local language. Surely I could teach village women such basic concepts!

---

[14]   Post-partum hemorrhage, a common cause of death after delivery, is often caused by either retention of part of the placenta, or failure of the uterus to contract, allowing profuse bleeding which rapidly results in death of the mother, and later, without a source of nutrition, the child. The *sasura* will not touch the placenta or perform uterine massage, and did not want me to touch anything as it was considered unclean.

[15]   *Obstructed labor* refers to a delivery where either the position of the baby does not allow delivery or the mother's birth canal cannot accommodate the child. Fetal distress is a term used to denote a baby's difficulty during the labor process, which when left unaddressed leads to lack of oxygen and death of the neonate.

I enlisted the help of Jonequi, our inherited house helper and the village gossip, as chief planner and organizer. We bought a hanging scale, an ingenious bag suspended from a hook in the ceiling that could accurately weigh young children, and acquired unused height and weight growth cards for children under five years of age from the partially closed government health post. Jonequi recruited women from the surrounding area who were interested, or who just wanted to be where there was action. It was an exciting day of teaching basic information about pregnancy and childbirth, proper nutrition for mother and baby, and other simple antenatal information.

After my first "class" of about fifty women and their numerous children, I collapsed in hopeful exhaustion into a wooden chair in our tiny, crowded kitchen. Jonequi and I discussed the success of our health outreach, but at the end of our conversation I realized a sad truth; even she still did not understand the most rudimentary concepts. Very little of what I taught had made any sense to her. Though she had attended the project's literacy class, I later learned that the teacher never actually came to class, so she and the other students were paid a fee to attend but never learned to read or write. Her eyes were not opened first by literacy, and thus she could not understand simple concepts such as the germ theory. This failure on my part allowed us to recognize the need to train national colleagues who had appropriate education, to take information and deliver it in a way that could be understood by less educated, but intelligent, locals.

Recognizing our inability to transmit information effectively, partially due to our *excessive* education, cultural background, and methods of learning, was a humbling lesson that provided a key step in H.E.L.P. program development. Once we began to see how the local people thought and reasoned, we could use our educational perspective and methods more effectively to communicate ideas in trainer-of-trainer programs rather than the rote educational method that was typically used. The strategy of training a local person to teach others became a key part of H.E.L.P.'s success.

Our Cultural Education

While life in the village was an amazing learning experience, it was hard. There were no stores and nominally fresh vegetables were available at the market only once a week. We planted a garden, but soon learned that gardens were considered community property unless protected by thorns; much of what we planted was eaten by our neighbors or their animals. The perception that we were rich foreigners led our neighbors to feel justified to steal whatever they could secretly take. While we considered the fact that we had given up all our worldly goods, great jobs and incomes, and sacrificed to serve the people, the villagers saw us as rich Americans who—even when living in the village—had extra clothes, enough food, toys for our children, and books! Recognizing these reactions helped us avoid bitterness and anger toward those who did not always demonstrate gratitude to us, especially when we felt we had sacrificed so much. Christ left his heavenly home and humbled himself, so why should it be so difficult for us to survive with a bit less luxury?

One morning, I searched for the plastic washbasin I used to wash our dishes and discovered that Hajur-Ama was using it in her hut. Since the running water frequently did not run, and we had no hot water, we had to boil water both for drinking and for washing clothes or dishes. To wash, I diluted the boiled water with the cold, added soap, and washed our dishes in a large plastic tub. The tub cost about two dollars in the market. I felt too embarrassed to confront Hajur-Ama with the obvious thievery, so I asked Jonequi to retrieve it.

"She knew you could buy another, and just borrowed it until you needed it," Jonequi reported.

Frequently, there was no electricity. The only way to light a mud house with no electricity is to open the shutters over the windows. We had the benefit of screens, which lowered the population of flies from the neighboring water buffalo wallow, but the open shutters meant our family provided live entertainment for our neighbors in an area where television and movies were not available. Each meal was observed by as many crowded faces as could peer into our window. With all the interruptions, homeschooling was an incredible challenge. Mounds of termites, which could eat a page in a school book overnight, distracted our two older children from their reading.

The children, however, received a cultural education that deeply impacted them. Kalpana was a little girl Kristen's age that lived in a hut next door, and they often played together. Because one side of the house was open to our window, we saw and heard everything. Even at age six, Kristen was shocked at the family's treatment of Kalpana; she was punished if her little brother fell down, or if misfortune befell him. If food was limited, her brother ate a full meal, but Kalpana's mother did not feed her; therefore, Kalpana often snuck over to our home for food. Here, in the school of life, we saw the destructive factors of illiteracy and the caste system resulting in the oppression of women, even encouraging women to discriminate against their own daughters by giving the best food and care to their sons. This impact was so strong in the memory of our daughter that in high school she wrote a short composition, "Kalpana's Story," about the tragedy of this little girl's life.

The real education came when another neighbor decided to sell her thirteen-year-old orphaned relative as a second wife to my friend's husband. Dhana Kumari, a gentle, beautiful woman of about thirty, was "cursed" with having three daughters. When she was pregnant with her fourth child, a local shaman (witch doctor) told her husband the baby would be another girl. Determined to have a son, of vital importance for Hindu rituals and culture, her husband decided to marry a second wife. A cheap, pretty one was available in the village— our neighbor's orphaned relative. When Dhana Kumari told me, I was furious. Not only was it against the law, it was morally wrong and even dangerous, as the girl was so young. To magnify the crime, her husband was purchasing the girl with money Dhana Kumari earned working! Determined to stick to the law and fight against an oppressive culture as Christ would do, we decided to help Dhana Kumari in her plight. She felt paralyzed: if she turned her husband into the police and he divorced her, she would have no way to earn money; culturally it was unacceptable to return to her parent's home. Her husband worked on the same hydropower project, under Tim's division, so we were sure Tim could have him fired if he persisted in this decision. Tim wrote a letter to the higher management explaining the situation.

"We're sorry, however, we cannot interfere in personal matters," was the response.

"What if I took a second wife?" he asked. "Would you terminate my position?"

"That is a different situation," said the mission director, suggesting that we lived by a different set of laws. He, in his double standard and failure to defend the defenseless, demonstrated worse hypocrisy and lack of spiritual depth than the local police, who for a small bribe simply ignored the polygamy and child marriage forbidden by national law. This was the nominally Christian mission agency with which we later had further disagreements, and from whom God separated us in order to effectively develop H.E.L.P.'s ministry.

Over the ensuing months, I recognized the fatalistic mentality and acceptance of poverty, death, and disease as part of the villagers' perception of *karma*. This was a huge battle that simple education could never defeat. In the Hindu and Buddhist *dharma* (religion), *karma* (fate) is what you earn, based on the deeds of your previous life. If you are good in your life, you will be incarnated at a higher level, and if you are evil, at a lower level. This also determines the *caste* (family tribe) into which you are born. The Brahman caste (the priests) are the highest, while the Untouchables are the lowest. Marriage, eating, drinking, delivery of babies, and medical care are all determined by caste. For most village

> *Ke Garne* is a common Nepali phrase that literally means "what to do?" and indicates the frustration and hopelessness people feel toward the seemingly inescapable cycle of poverty and hardship.

women, illiterate and oppressed, the idea that they can change the outcome of their lives and the lives of their children is unthinkable until the blindness of illiteracy and fatalism is lifted. People reared in this type of culture—especially those who are uneducated—simply accept life without attempting to change it.[16]

With few modern distractions, village life might have been idyllic, but the reality was that life for most was hard and food was difficult to grow. As in most societies, alcoholism and abuse accompanied poverty. Every village had a town drunk (or many), but our town drunk had a lovely wife who was, of course, my friend. She came to our porch for me to treat wounds and bandage cuts she received in beatings; I begged her to leave her cruel husband. Just like Dhana Kumari, she shared as she wept, "Didi (big sister), how can I leave? I am a poor woman. When I left my family to marry, I no longer have my family. I

---

[16]   This is a simplistic explanation of a difficult concept.

belong to my husband. I cannot read. I cannot write. I have no way to feed my children. I have to stay."

I resolved that if we could teach women how to read, write, and make money, they would not only be able to learn about the Savior, but also would win the respect of their husbands. If their husbands continued to mistreat them, then they would have the option to make it on their own! The insights gained from our friends helped us understand the importance of women's literacy, informal education, and income generation. We also recognized that the transformational power of the gospel is more effective than laws or social taboos in effecting community change. As we struggled to understand the minds of our neighbors by relating to their worldview, culture, and language, we also sought friendships from fellow-workers in the gospel in other parts of the country and region. These included Bible translators, literacy experts, health workers, and agriculturalists from a variety of Christian denominations. They willingly shared years of experience, which enabled us to learn from mistakes and successes of other pioneers in a land where the gospel was just beginning to penetrate. Their wisdom proved invaluable and, in later times of trial, these true friends encouraged us to persevere in Christ's service.

While I was attempting to balance my time between home, cultural learning, child care, and medical practice, Tim had his own sets of problems trying to be an environmental coordinator with a project that cared little about community development and a supervisor who expected falsified reports to the World Bank in order to receive more loans. One of his jobs was literacy supervision. In order to give back to the community, the project spent over two million dollars in literacy classes. Tim was determined to make sure the women of the area had a chance to improve their lives. However, after a few surprise visits to the classes, accompanied by his national colleagues, he realized that the project was paying many teachers, but few were showing up to teach. In fact, after two years, only two women out of the hundreds who supposedly had completed the class could even write their names! This invaluable experience paved the road toward a more effective literacy program with excellent quality control for H.E.L.P.

As with any big construction project in the Himalayas, poor laborers migrate into "labor camps" to carry stones and sacks of supplies on their back. The tiny mountain trails do not permit vehicles, so supplies are carried painstakingly on the backs of sweating laborers, much like army ants carrying food along a path single-file. As the community development director, Tim received reports of major occurrences among the labor camps. On one occasion he received news that a wave of dysentery and death was affecting laborers. The newly hired national project doctor had just arrived after completing medical school in Russia. The young man tried to send some antibiotics, but did not know what to do. Immediately after Tim received the news, he struck out to investigate the problem, hiking miles to reach the laborer villages. Knowing the unsanitary conditions, he delegated workers to build toilets[17] at all tea shops,[18] and sent the thirty national workers in his department to provide hygiene training to the shop owners. This stopped the cholera epidemic, but it caused us to wonder why the project's new national doctor had simply dispensed medicine at the start of the epidemic. We recognized that, unfortunately, even the more educated do not always understand simple, effective means of

---

[17] Pit latrines are simple outhouses made with a deep hole surrounded by bamboo or stones. Once it is full of human excrement, the hole can be covered and the outhouse moved. In rural areas materials for septic tanks are unavailable, and even a simple outhouse is unusual.

[18] Small shacks that typically have minimal, if any, hygiene, and serve tea and snacks.

preventing disease and death, because they lack understanding of the basics of public health.

Our next public health education and development lesson came from Bharat. On a hike to survey one of the project sites, Tim saw a young boy of about ten with a bandaged hand. Turning to his co-worker, he asked the cause of the child's injury. His colleague explained, "Our new project power lines have just gone up. They have a sign warning people not to touch the lines, but no one can read them. This boy was probably sent up the lines to hook in and get power for his house. He touched the power lines and was electrocuted."

Miraculously, Bharat did not die, but his hand and arm were already black with gangrene from the electric burn. The medical assistant at a distant government health post had simply wrapped the hand with gauze. Bharat soon came to our home. After treating his dry gangrene and visiting with his parents, we convinced the project to help fund the cost of amputation of his arm and rehabilitation. During this time he stayed with a Nepali pastor friend, and as a result of this family's witness, Bharat gave his life to Christ. Bharat's experience illustrated a mismatch of the world's definition of development. Propelling developing countries into the modern era without taking initial steps toward literacy with education can be devastating to individuals and communities.

Mounting Trials

One day, Judy and I were seeing children at the under-fives clinic when the nurse midwife brought in an extremely malnourished child, Jamuna. It was a typical story—her mother could not deliver, and her father used his resources to take her to the closest health facility, a small simple clinic manned by a minimally trained health worker. Though Jamuna was finally born, the health worker did not recognize that her mother had twins. On the way home, the mother died in obstructed labor with the twin, leaving Jamuna to be wet-nursed by any willing village woman. By a year of age she weighed a mere eight pounds. She was unable to sit up, and lay, lethargic, on a blanket full of diarrheal stool. I asked her father if we could nurse her for a while, and suggested he send her older sister to stay in our mud home, realizing the child would otherwise not live. Living with us, she perked up quickly, and within a week, Jamuna was bright-eyed and her older sister had sufficiently explored our house to steal all the items she could hide in her sari.

While we searched for an adoptive family (at her father's request) our children endeavored to entertain Jamuna. We found a plastic baby toy, and two-year-old Austin, our youngest, accidentally threw the toy toward Kristen as she was swinging on the swing we had rigged in the field by our house (enjoyed by the entire village). Kristen began crying and ran to me, saying: "Mommy, I can't see anything." Thinking she was exaggerating, I grabbed my ophthalmoscope and examining her eye, saw a large traumatic hyphema.[19] The nearest eye hospital was a day's bus ride away, and there were no buses. It was dusk, a dangerous time to travel on treacherous mountain roads, but I decided to go in the only available vehicle in the area, the project "ambulance." Kristen was still recovering from a broken arm,[20] suffered when Aaron had pushed her off the bed in a tussle over a book. To make matters worse, I fell and severely sprained my ankle in my hurry across uneven terrain

---

[19] A hyphema is blood in the anterior chamber of the eye, which indicates trauma to the eye globe. It can cause loss of vision, as well as blindness if the excessive pressure on the optic nerve is not relieved within 24 hours.

[20] She sustained a supra-condylar fracture, which can damage the growth plate and cause the arm to grow abnormally. This accident had required another emergency trip into Kathmandu and a different harrowing journey.

of rice paddy fields. Though the pain was intense, I managed to hobble to the car, where Kristen nestled her head in my lap, arm still in a cast.

The next eight hours were harrowing. The driver, tired from working all day, nearly fell asleep at the wheel, and while I was trying to elevate my ankle and keep Kristen's head still to avoid increased intraocular (eye) pressure, I continually talked to him, grabbing the wheel on several occasions when we were headed off the edge of the mountain road. I was six months pregnant and the curvy roads in the dark combined with the intense ankle pain were overwhelming.

When we finally arrived at the eye hospital in the early morning, we found a resident doctor who was unable to help. He simply touched Kristen's eyelids, glanced at her eye, and announced with confidence: "Your daughter has a hyphema." By late morning, we were desperate and called some close friends living in Kathmandu. They invited us to stay with them and assisted us in finding a well-trained ophthalmologist. He followed Kristen's eye pressures closely, treating the hyphema; by God's grace she had a complete recovery from the hyphema, as well as normal function of her arm.

Meanwhile, in the village, Tim was managing his job, our other children, our foster baby, her thieving sister, and a visiting couple who were hoping to adopt Jamuna. At this difficult time, trials continued to mount. Unknown to us, Satan intended to destroy our family and prevent the development of H.E.L.P.

While our family was undergoing these trials and spiritual attacks, the political situation was becoming more and more tense. Our district was completely controlled by the Maoist Communists, and our only communication station was blown up. We had almost no communication by phone, email, or fax, and rarely even by mail. Unsure whether any of our prayer partners other than my mother remembered us, we felt intense stress. Nationally, people were unhappy, as faith in the king was lessening and many no longer viewed him as an incarnation of the god Vishnu. We continued to learn more and more about village life in a poor farming society and the personal hardships families endured. We had other close calls with the children. Aaron, our wandering child, could disappear within two minutes. A blue-eyed cotton-topped child, he stood out, but the question, "Have you seen our child?" was usually answered by a Nepali farmer: "That direction." We learned that though spoken in confidence, it was culturally unacceptable to say, "I don't know," so we generally chose the opposite direction to search for Aaron. On one occasion, Austin grabbed Aaron's asthma medicine—which had potential cardiac (heart) toxicity—and drank it. On other occasions, both Aaron and Austin suffered severe asthma attacks.

One night, Aaron was particularly ill from an allergy to the blooming rice plants. We had not had electricity for some time in our home, and Tim had to walk a mile to the project headquarters, where there was some electricity, to charge batteries for the nebulizer.[21] There was no oxygen anywhere, and I knew if Aaron stopped breathing or became hypoxic[22] there would be nothing we could do. We prayed, gave him continual treatments all night, and God delivered him. Later, we had several similar experiences with Austin's croup, but God was gracious and healed him.

These were incredibly trying times, especially to me as both a mother and a physician. I experienced, even as a doctor, the helplessness that the village women knew so well and accepted as unchangeable *karma*. So many of the women I treated as patients,

---

[21] A nebulizer is used to aerosolize asthma medication to deliver it effectively to young children, in particular.

[22] Hypoxia is low oxygen in the blood (which can result from severe asthma) leading to death.

and shared with as friends, had suffered the loss of multiple children. Christ gave me a gift of compassion, which grew into a determination to help these families overcome their fatalistic mentality based on a circle of reincarnation that they strongly believed was inescapable. The desperate and difficult conditions we witnessed and experienced deeply influenced the development of H.E.L.P. God, in His grace, did spare our children. Not only that, he allowed us to experience incarnational missions in a way that most modern-day foreign missionaries do not have the opportunity to experience.

Biblical Principles:

1. *Jesus is the perfect example of incarnational missions—he became like us and identified with us.*

   He "made himself nothing, by taking the very nature of a servant, being made in human likeness . . . humbled himself by becoming obedient to death" (Philippians 2:7-8). In the same way, in order to identify with a people group, a community, or a nation, we must live like them as much as possible and learn their culture and language. Though Americans may not consider themselves wealthy, even our poor are rich compared to those living in many poverty-stricken areas of the world. In addition, the movie industry and media have painted a picture of our culture that leads many to perceive Americans are all wealthy and immoral. Before we can offer the good news of Christ, we must be an asset to a community and a friend to the locals, understanding their needs and perceptions.

2. *Incarnational missions, especially for a family with young children, can be dangerous and difficult.*

   Many long-term missionaries justify living at a higher standard, and in a more developed area, in order to be able to stay longer on the field. While this is certainly understandable, living in the community allowed us to better understand those we are serving, just as Jesus can intercede for us because He lived among us. Those considering serving in difficult areas must count the cost (Luke 14:28).

Chapter 3

Birth Pains

Authority Abused

Near the end of the hydropower project, shortly after many of our health trials, we endured perhaps the greatest trial up to that point. This trial, however, led to great success in God's kingdom. For us, it was truly a validation of Romans 8:28:

> *"And we know that all things work together for good to them that love God, to them who are the called according to His purpose."* (KJV)

While we were struggling with the children's illnesses, extra people in our tiny home, and daily stresses, Tim continued to be verbally attacked by a difficult high-caste Brahmin Nepali supervisor. He officially had five different directors on the field, in the capital, and through the umbrella organization, as well as the sending mission organization through which our donors and home church sent support. This sending mission also had a supervising pastoral care based in Thailand, but these pastors barely knew us. Unfortunately, none of these five men communicated, and the expatriate supervisor in the capital who was most connected to the actual project (and our friend) was tragically killed in a rafting accident. The civil war was escalating, and we felt the children were not safe in our remote village location. Finally, Tim decided to resign his position with the hydropower project, which was now nearly completed. We were discouraged, and we did not know how the Lord would use us, but we knew we could not stay in the same position or continue to work with the same organizations. We thought it would be best for Tim to resign his position because of increased hostility and altercations with his Nepali supervisor. The very same day on which Tim resigned, we received information from my mother that after nearly two years of delays, the IRS had approved Health Environmental and Learning Program (H.E.L.P.) as an official 501 (c)(3) nonprofit organization. The timing was a direct answer from God, an almost audible voice from Him said, *"Don't give up, this is just the beginning." "Those who go out weeping, carrying seed to sow, will return with songs of joy, carrying sheaves with them." Psalm 126:6*

While I, too, was approaching the time of birth for our fourth child, God in his sovereignty decided it was time for H.E.L.P.'s official birth. A few days after Tim's resignation, the mission agency which processed our financial support within the umbrella organization in Nepal—as well as our main supporting home church—received and believed false information about his resignation. Initially, the agency's pastoral representative flew in from Thailand (at our expense), and demanded that due to our insubordination to the mission's authority, we must immediately leave our village home. We, our team at the hydropower project, and our neighbors were shocked. He did not follow accepted cultural norms or even simple courtesy towards our family, avoiding discussion with those most closely associated with our work. We were already overwhelmed by the anticipation of moving from our village home due to our resignation from Tim's position, and as I was nearing the end of my pregnancy, were preparing to return to the United States for our child's delivery.

Relieved that our main supporting church had previously planned to send an elder and missions pastor to visit us, we looked forward to good fellowship and clarification of issues. We had been married in that church, had worked side-by-side for years in growing the church's international ministry, and had led home fellowship groups for years. To our surprise, instead of joining us in visiting areas of outreach, the missions pastor, his wife, and an elder enjoyed souvenir shopping, sightseeing, a hairdressing appointment, and meetings with the personnel director. Unfortunately, however, the personnel director with the umbrella mission in Nepal had placed false information in our file and claimed we were unwilling to submit to his "authority." Several months after our resignation, he was removed from his position due to serious psychological and spiritual issues, a confirmation of our right standing. Nevertheless, decisions were based on his information and circulated email hearsay. In our time of deepest discouragement and need, the elder and pastor, our "friends", told us that we were "insubordinate and unresponsive to leadership." Once again, none of the church or mission leadership directly discussed issues with our national colleagues, mission coworkers in the village, or even with us! The children, suddenly uprooted from their village home and friends, struggled to cope. Tim felt a failure in his work, and with the effects of stress, poor nutrition, and third-trimester pregnancy, I contracted a serious case of influenza (flu). This, combined with condemnation from those we thought had supported and believed in the vision God gave us, nearly led us to despair.

Reeling from change, exhaustion, and self-condemnation, we received one final call hours before boarding a plane to take a three-day journey back to the United States. We had left our possessions in a Nepali storage facility, which was owned by the umbrella mission. They informed us that the personnel director said we could not keep anything there and must make other arrangements. Thankfully, the kind Hindu Nepali in charge recognized the impossibility of moving our belongings at the last minute and ignored the mandate, which had been given by the personnel director in a spirit of vindictiveness.

Less than two weeks before our scheduled departure, through the referral of a friend who was involved in Bible translation, the Lord allowed us to meet an enterprising Nepali doctor establishing a community hospital. The doctor requested my assistance in caring for patients and developing the hospital's health care program for women and children. The location was in a more developed region of Nepal (still quite rural) and in the same town as a university where Tim and I could both be involved in educating students in our respective fields. The hospital promised the possibility of a visa, lodging, and a contract when we returned after my delivery. Unsure whether this vague possibility of a new position would materialize, we left Nepal to return to the United States discouraged, wondering if God had a plan.

The trip home was much more difficult than before. Where previously we had been filled with hope, now we were nearly hopeless. We had almost no money, and we slept during layovers in airport lobbies, settling the kids in our arms. Despite these hardships and rejection, we felt God somehow *had* a plan that we did not see.[23] Soon after our arrival back home for my delivery, the supervising mission, along with the pastor and elders of our main sending church, took a step further to ensure we would not return to the field. They wrote to us stating, "If you return to the mission field against our advice, without at least one year of counseling, we will permanently terminate fellowship with you." The letter went on to exhort that if we went against their spiritual authority, God might even punish us by taking

---

[23] Several years later, a number of prayer supporters shared stories of how God brought us into their minds and prayers during this time, though they were unaware of our circumstances. One even had a vivid dream at the exact time, in which he saw demonic attacks intended to cause us to give up.

the lives of our children, a threat that seemed only too real after our experiences. Just two weeks from delivering our daughter Kayla, crushed and angry at the cruel attacks, I claimed the promises in Job 23:10, "But He knows the way that I take, and when he has tested me, I shall come forth as gold" and Psalms 37:6, "He will make your righteousness shine like the dawn, your vindication like the noonday sun." God heard our desperate prayers. He reminded us that H.E.L.P. was born at the exact time we had resigned—and His timing was perfect.

Working for Good

Within two months of arriving home, God brought together our supporters, close friends, and the pastor and leaders of my parents' church (the church we had joined prior to our departure to Nepal) to pray and officially begin developing H.E.L.P. These amazing, godly men and women provided the finances, prayer support, and spiritual guidance we needed, just when those we thought were our friends and spiritual leaders had turned their backs on us. Now, instead of returning as professionals under a nominally Christian mission, we would return as professionals working through our own mission agency. We would have the freedom to develop the program we believed God wanted with much more flexibility than if we were with a traditional mission or a completely secular organization. The Lord forcibly kicked us off one path and onto a better one He designed. He provided a work visa and free housing, moving us into one of the most beautiful and best localities for both a ministry center and H.E.L.P. headquarters. We could not have chosen a more ideal location if we had known!

What Satan meant for our destruction, God instead used to begin a ministry that has brought and is bringing physical and spiritual deliverance to thousands—with God as chief architect. His plan to show a *better* way to plant sustainable churches without external dependency (through Christian community development) was not thwarted by pastors and leaders claiming His guidance!

Incidentally, Kayla LeNelle was born without complications, and I had far less birth pain in labor than we had in the birth of H.E.L.P.! She smiled for her first passport photo at one week of age. By six weeks of age, she—along with our other three children—was on her way back to a new home in the Himalayas, where I would serve as a family medicine doctor and maternal-child director of a community hospital and later assist in starting and teaching in a medical school. Tim would help with home school and teach environmental sciences at the local university. On the side, we would develop H.E.L.P. using the experiences in relationships, knowledge, and humility God was teaching us. Even with all of our shortcomings, God chose to use our lives given as a living sacrifice (Romans 12:1) to bring Him glory.

We clearly saw the Lord's hand of direction in our lives just as Joseph, sold by his own brothers as a slave but brought to great power and influence by God, realized:

> *You intended to harm me, but God intended it for good to accomplish what is now being done, the saving of many lives.* Genesis 50:20

God was removing all we depended on and was truly conforming us to the likeness of his Son:

> *For we are God's handiwork, created in Christ Jesus to do good works, which God prepared in advance for us to do.* Ephesians 2:10

We could never have done and could never continue doing the good works God created for us to do through H.EL.P. if we had not returned to the Himalayas. He wanted to give our family the privilege of trials, joys, and suffering in order to develop a Christian community development program to help those in spiritual and physical poverty to live abundantly. Satan nearly had victory at this dark time in our lives:

> But thanks be to God! He gives us the victory through our Lord Jesus Christ. I Corinthians 15:57

Biblical Principles:

1. *Spiritual authority can be abused.*
   Those in leadership in the church must be careful to correct only for sin, but not be instruments for division and discouragement. Throughout church history, religion (not necessarily a true relationship with Christ) has been a source of political intrigue and abuse of power. Rumors and third-party sources are unreliable and should not be used to make decisions. Particularly in areas of great spiritual warfare, where the gospel is just beginning to penetrate, Satan will use divisiveness and discouragement to ruin those soldiers on the front lines. In our case, as in many, the misunderstanding and poor handling of conflict could have resulted in a tragedy. While those in authority in the church deserve our respect, we must interpret their advice and teaching with the scripture, and when they conflict, we must obey God rather than man (Acts 5:29). Ultimately, we all have to answer to God for our decisions and actions. Leaders, pastors, and elders in the church, however, must be especially careful in handling issues on the foreign field. Spiritual and personal accountability for Christian aid workers, "tentmakers", or traditional missionaries is critical, but criticism when facts are unclear and the spiritual counselors know do not understand the culture or situation can lead to

divisiveness and harm the gospel. Those in leadership have a greater responsibility and will be judged more harshly (James 3:1).

2. *In all things, God "works for the good of those who love him, who have been called according to his purpose" (Romans 8:28).*

Sometimes what we see as the best way, He realizes will not work, and the pain we endure is simply the suffering before the harvest (Psalm 126:6). What was initially intense pain and a time of great suffering, God used to begin the "good work" He desired for His glory.

Chapter 4

Seeing Needs and Building Relationships

Return to Nepal

Our return to Nepal was quite different from the previous trip. Rather than fending for ourselves in an unkempt mission guest house in Kathmandu, we were graciously met at the airport by one of the employees of the Nepali community hospital where I would be serving, and driven to a lovely town two hours east of the capital. After the painful experience with our original sending church and the nominally Christian supervisory organization, we were hesitant to make ties with any traditional Christian mission agencies or expatriate missionaries, though there were none in our area, anyway. We were now volunteers with H.E.L.P., working to develop this hospital's programs and teaching in the local university; we were working directly with the Nepalese with no intermediary administration. This decision to distance ourselves from any Christian mission organization also freed us from local and governmental suspicion and prejudices, allowing us to develop deeper friendships with our neighbors and other professionals, and to demonstrate our commitment to the local community.

Our tiny apartment, a second-floor flat of nearly 600 square feet, accommodated our family of six, plus occasional guests. There were no doors between our flat and the neighbors'; thankfully, we became close friends. It did present problems, however, when their goats and chickens wandered up the stairs, or when the little boy from downstairs stole our children's toys. The flat roof with a two-foot parapet around the edge was large enough for us to rig a semi-safe swing set and grow a few plants in pots, from which the prettiest flowers were unfortunately plucked by our neighbor for *puja* to the Hindu gods. Our children were especially excited to have small shops down the street, with shopkeepers who loved giving the only towheaded kids in town pieces of gum and candy. More frequent running water and electricity, as well as a proper indoor western-style flush toilet (which sometimes had enough water to flush), all made for easier adjustments than life in a small, remote village. (Fig 3.1-3.4)

During the first few years of my work at the community hospital, Tim was busy being a house-husband, schooling our older children, and building relationships in the town. When I could not escape the unending line of patients to ride my bicycle home to nurse Kayla, he walked several miles to bring her to me. At times, he even had to protect her from well-intended ladies who, upon hearing her cry, walked into our flat and offered to nurse her until I arrived home. Shortly after moving in, we heard there was a new college-preparatory private school with a British principal. Our deep desire was for our children to continue learning the local language and culture, but we were uncomfortable with the school's opening ceremony, which included prayers to idols. Though the school seemed suitable, Aaron, then five years old, was miserable because the other children loved touching his white hair and peering into his blue eyes. The English-speaking teachers who were supposed to help him with Nepali did not speak English well, so he crawled under his desk and refused to come out. Kristen fared slightly better; during the morning prayers she noticed two other girls besides her who did not pray to the idols, and she became fast friends with the sisters. Though after six weeks we decided to homeschool the children again, her friendship with these girls resulted in a lifelong partnership. Our families became best friends and their mother, Mrs. Bajracharya, later became H.E.L.P.'s national director.

My two years developing women's health and neonatal care at the community hospital proved priceless. Though a family physician, I primarily functioned as a consultant in obstetrics and gynecology, as well as in pediatrics and any other difficult diagnostic cases in other specialties. Night call was 24-7, as needed. As we had no phone, the ambulance would arrive below our window, honk the horn, and race me to the hospital. My frequent night visits on foot had ended after near-disastrous attacks by wild dogs. Patients arrived with everything from simple infections to complicated rheumatic heart disease during pregnancy. I was able to learn firsthand of many heartbreaking tragedies, and I examined and treated shameful medical problems such as uterine prolapse,[24] which many believed to be incurable.[25] Nurse midwives handled the few simple deliveries we saw; most uncomplicated deliveries took place in the home. Clinic days were interrupted countless times by adrenaline-pumping delivery cases. Stretchers bearing women in active labor with thick meconium,[26] eclampsia,[27] infection, and other life-threatening pregnancy

---

[24]   A condition that often results from long, obstructive labor and poor nutrition, in which the uterus protrudes through the opening of the vagina, causing pain and urinary obstruction.

[25]   Though not legal, polygamy is commonly practiced, especially in rural areas. Because women with complete uterine prolapse have difficulty with sexual relations or bearing more children, it is common for them to become the second (lesser) wife when their husband marries another woman.

[26]   Amniotic fluid with waste passed by the fetus due to intrauterine stress.

[27]   Seizures caused by high blood pressure of pregnancy.

complications challenged my attempts to see lines of women who often traveled days to be examined.

Working in a completely indigenous setting, administered and directed by passionate and intelligent nationals of a different faith, gave me a completely different experience from what I had seen in traditional Christian mission hospitals in Ecuador, Bangladesh, and Ghana. These outstanding mission hospitals provided curative care to the poor through dedicated expatriate missionaries serving in health professions. But Tim and I envisioned a new model, a wholistic approach in which we had a backseat role, inspiring by example, teaching, and building local capacity.

These experiences also allowed me to see the needs of people and recognize, once again, the critical nature of addressing disease early. My daily activities seemed endless. Between seeing hundreds of patients, supervising recently graduated medical doctors, teaching students, and handling complicated deliveries and newborn emergencies, I enjoyed the opportunity to both learn from and teach my colleagues. To improve care, I developed a local version of emergency obstetrics and pediatric resuscitations in Nepali, and taught nurse midwives working in surrounding districts with our hospital. Later, we invited some American physicians to teach emergency courses for obstetric and pediatric care, Advanced Life Support in Obstetrics (ALSO), and a modified version of Pediatric Advanced Life Support (PALS), alongside our Nepali colleagues.

Cooperative relationships were critical—we never had a superior role. Instead, we taught together and learned from one another. National physicians embraced the curriculum and ideas, adapted it to fit their needs, and continued the programs in a way that suited their local culture.

Most of the patients were casualties from simple illnesses easily preventable by community interventions, but some situations embedded in my mind dramatic needs that we determined to meet as H.E.L.P. developed. These experiences clarified to us the importance of community-based interventions as our emphasis, and the reinforcement of our belief that wholistic spiritual and physical health is multifactorial.

Stories from Hospital Experiences

Pasang, a cute little boy from a remote village in the eastern part of Nepal, was brought to the hospital by his grandfather. His father had died and his mother abandoned him, leaving his grandfather with yet another mouth to feed. Pasang weighed barely 20 pounds at four years of age and had a distended stomach. After some testing and examinations, I diagnosed him with intestinal tuberculosis—a common disease caused by ingesting unpasteurized milk from diseased animals. As I explained the need to stay in the hospital for a few days because there were no anti-tuberculosis medication programs in his district and Pasang's disease was severe, his grandfather explained: "I must go; if I stay, I cannot plant the fields and the whole family will starve."

His story, as well as others, emphasized the role of animals in human disease, as well as the relationship between food availability and health. Though, in theory, there was a directly observed therapy (DOT) tuberculosis program in the country, inaccessibility of care coupled with lack of infrastructure made it non-existent in his area. The complex nature of health was on display. First, Pasang contracted his disease from an infected animal. Second, his grandfather needed a trained health worker locally to administer medication and ensure compliance with the many months of therapy. Last, his poor nutritional status was worsened by lack of food availability, a problem facing nearly every family in this country based on subsistent agriculture.

On another occasion, a local diphtheria epidemic was caused by infected goat's milk and a combination of ineffective or nonexistent immunization of the goats and the children. Even in areas where immunization was available, lack of electricity led to poor storage and made vaccines ineffective. The health of the animals quite often directly affects the health of the family to whom they belong, as families and animals live together. To change the health of thousands like Pasang (or the children who died in the diphtheria epidemic) we needed more than immunizations—we needed a program to help families like his to prevent illness in or treat the diseased animals. In addition, Pasang's grandfather had no cash with which to purchase food if he could not work. His community needed a means to grow animals to both eat and sell for income, and improved agriculture methods to have extra food to store or sell.

Maya arrived in the clinic in septic shock[28]—nearly dead, with one hand of her deceased baby protruding. She was an example of an all too common complication, transverse lie.[29] Unfortunately, in many areas of the Himalayas, there is no access to care for operative obstetrics and most deliveries are in the home or a goat shed. Depending on their caste, women may deliver alone or be delivered by a mother-in-law. Traditional birth attendants are available in some

---

[28]   Septic shock refers to collapse of the circulatory system due to overwhelming infection. In her case, it was the rotting body of the deceased infant that could not deliver naturally.

[29]   Describes the position of the baby in the mother's womb (uterus) that is transverse, or horizontal. The infant cannot deliver, and without operative delivery, both mother and infant die.

areas and may be accepted in the case of a problem delivery. Many Himalayan regions have the highest maternal mortality in the world, as well as high infant death rates. In far west Nepal, the average life expectancy for women in some areas is still only 36 years. Maya was lucky—she made it to the hospital after her family walked for three days to carry her there, and though her baby died, she survived.

I was heartbroken when she told me: "Doctor, *Didi*, my husband will now need a second wife."

It had taken antibiotics, a hysterectomy, and three weeks of care to save her life. But now, she could not bear children. Due to medical expenses, she had unintentionally caused the poverty of her family, who now would have no money for food, and because she could no longer bear children, she would become a virtual slave to another woman. Another patient, Dolma, recovered in the hospital only to return to her village and commit suicide because of the shame of being unable to bear children. These women and thousands more, needed committed, compassionate Christian women who could assist in the birth process and diagnose problems like transverse lie prior to labor. They also needed alternative means to earn a living and a sense of self-worth only possible through learning to read and write.

Dechen was only in her thirties. Like most laborers, she worked hard in the field barefoot, wearing her flip-flops only for special occasions. She stepped on a thorn while planting crops, but ignored the wound for days. Her foot became swollen and red. Before coming in to the clinic, she tried remedies recommended by the local shaman (witch doctor). Finally, her foot became discolored and she came in for evaluation. It was too late—gangrene had set in and a simple wound that would have been curable with first aid had progressed to the point that it required total amputation of her foot. Clearly, there needed to be local leaders—Christian village health workers trained in the basis of sanitation, first aid, wound cleaning, treatment of simple worm infestations, and basic health concepts—who could treat simple wounds like hers and prevent the ensuing disability.

Lam came on a stretcher, carried by his family from the high mountains near Tibet. Many had died in his village in a typhoid epidemic, and he arrived with severe abdominal pain. Like others who never came to the hospital, he had complications of *salmonella typhi*, a bacteria spread through unclean food and water contaminated with feces. When we opened his abdomen, it was full of pus and innumerable intestinal perforations.[30] Clean water and use of toilets could have saved the lives of his neighbors and prevented the typhoid epidemic and his illness. Though the hospital team helped him, only an intervention at the community level could have changed the outcome for most of his family and friends who could not afford the transportation costs or died before treatment.

Having lived in a village and seen the smoke-filled kitchens where most women spend their lives, it was no surprise to me that by age thirty, many of my female patients had symptoms as severe as American patients have after thirty years of cigarette smoking. Women spent all day collecting firewood to cook the family's *daal bhaat* (rice and lentils). While attempting to gather firewood by cutting branches high in the tree, Leela fell, fracturing her lower vertebrae and suffering paralysis. Two-year-old Norbu and his siblings huddled around a fire to stay warm in their hut, but when no one was watching, he fell and rolled into the fire. His mother managed to rescue him, but after a three-day walk to the clinic, we had to amputate part of his arm to prevent his death. In addition, years of cutting trees for firewood, combined with slash-and-burn agriculture techniques, resulted in

---

[30]   Holes or openings in the intestine, which if not treated and repaired, lead to death.

major environmental issues. Each monsoon season, thousands lost their homes or lives in landslides resulting from deforestation. Others had no roads on which to access a market for their farm produce or travel by bus to a clinic for health care. These families needed a more efficient cooking method that conserved wood, a fireplace or stove to prevent accidental burns, and a method of decreasing deforestation. They needed a *duwa rahit chulo*.[31]

Parbati, a friend and neighbor, tried to keep her house clean and free from flies. One hot afternoon, her husband banged on our door: "Didi, my wife is unconscious and I think she could be poisoned."

Indeed, when we arrived in her kitchen, she was lying comatose with a can of organophosporous insecticide on the counter. She had used her hand to sprinkle the compound in her kitchen with the door and windows shut, accidentally poisoning herself with the locally available insecticide. We witnessed weekly suicide attempts with these dangerous compounds in the emergency department. Daily, I saw farmers suffering from neuropathy and other side effects from inappropriate pesticide use. Despite their attempts to reap better harvests on small plots of land that decreased in size with each successive generation, these farmers often poisoned themselves, their families, and those who ate their produce. Tim found that most farmers were not even using proper composting techniques. With the mountains, deforestation, loss of topsoil, and lack of crop rotation, the worn-out soil deteriorated further. These families needed effective,

---

[31]   Literally, a smokeless stove. One of a variety of types of "fireplaces" or "stoves" with chimneys that allow a small amount of wood or a charcoal brick to heat the pan with food more efficiently, protecting children from an open fire and funneling smoke through a hole in the mud wall for ventilation, as well as decreasing or eliminating the need for firewood.

pesticide-free organic farming techniques appropriate for their small plots of land and simple tools.

Hundreds of my pediatric patients—in fact, over 75 percent of all children under five years of age in the area—suffered from chronic malnutrition. Despite the combined efforts of myself and the hospital's nurse midwife who tirelessly worked with me to develop a nutritional program utilizing *sarbotam pitho*,[32] many of our patients' parents confessed that they simply did not have adequate food. All of the education we gave was useless because the food produced on the family land lasted less than twelve months of the year, leaving the children more susceptible to disease and death.[33] Only a program teaching parents how better utilize their land and increase production of vegetables and meat without the use of toxic pesticides could really change the health of the children. Handing out food was not the long-term answer.

Kanchi repeatedly came to the hospital clinic with her three children under five. All had multiple parasitic infections and despite my instructions to deworm them regularly, they suffered from malnutrition and recurrent diarrhea. Without basic literacy skills, Kanchi could not comprehend the need for good hygiene, and the connection between hand washing, bathing, and disease. Her husband had left for the Middle East in search of work, but though he had not sent money home for a year, she was burdened with his debt. Kanchi's children needed two things: literacy for their mother and economic

---

[32]   "Super-flour"—a mixture of ground soy, wheat, and other grains in a healthy combination for malnourished children.

[33]   Malnutrition, acute or chronic, affects the immune system contributing not only to retarded physical and mental growth, but also increased susceptibility to infectious disease.

alternatives for their father. The hospital and clinic could not provide these.

Two years of intensive work in the Nepali community hospitals taught me the limitations of the secondary and tertiary medical care available, how the private and government health system affected ability for patients in remote areas to access care, and the condition in which most patients arrived at hospital. In addition, I enjoyed teaching and learning from the nursing and medical students, nurses, midwives, and young doctors. Working closely at the hospital with nurse midwives trained in Nepal enabled me to later train our own H.E.L.P. midwife and health staff, recognizing their abilities and limitations. I also had the opportunity to conduct many medical camps as outreaches from the hospital to remote areas, train local nurse midwives in infant resuscitation and emergency obstetrics, and even visit and evaluate both government and private clinics providing basic care in rural areas. Without these experiences and exposure to the thousands of patients I treated, it would have been impossible to recognize the problems and their magnitude in a country of complicated social and religious constraints.

Because of close relationships Tim and I had built with a variety of Nepali friends and colleagues, as well as my work with the hospital, we were both asked to teach at the local university at the completion of our two-year contract. The university's new medical school needed experienced professors and I already had credentials from the United States, which helped fulfill their requirements for certification. In addition, they established an exchange program with an Ivy League medical school in the United States, and as a bilingual American professor, I could assist in improving communication between both sides of the faculty. After a brief visit home, we returned on a new visa post arrangement in which I would teach and develop courses for the medical school in the areas of physical diagnosis, history taking, and community health, while Tim would teach environmental science courses at the university and coach their basketball team. This was perfect for us, because we could share the responsibilities of homeschooling and had more opportunities to deepen friendships with professional colleagues as well as villagers. In addition, this finally gave us some time to work with and develop H.E.L.P. in our "free" time.

Some of my most interesting times on the medical school faculty were spent on field surveys and community health visits with medical students. Though the students were predominately upper middle class and had a limited understanding of their own country's development needs, their excitement to understand the villagers' lives inspired me. During a nutritional survey within an hour's travel to Kathmandu, we found children with night blindness from vitamin A deficiency living next door to a health post providing free vitamin A supplementation capsules funded through a prominent international non-governmental organization (INGO). In another survey we visited a village given money through a non-governmental organization (NGO) to build *duwa rahit chulos* to prevent burns and smoke-related diseases. The stoves were manufactured and had not been built by the locals, and none were functional only a year after the project ended. In addition, the money given for building the stoves was, instead, often used for materials to build stills to make *raksi* (local alcohol). On another community visit, we found beautiful brick toilets built by an INGO that were untouched and unused. The locals found them too nice to use as an outhouse. As they were more weather and rodent-proof than their village homes, families ingeniously used the outhouses to store grain. The INGO had failed to first educate the community about the *need* for the toilets, and then made the common mistake of building toilets for the people rather than simply teaching them and supervising

their own hard labor in building toilets. Tim and I studied programs—
some effective and others ineffective—designed to assist communities
to achieve a better standard of living and improved health measures,
taking notes to avoid the ineffective means. In addition, we were able
to examine data collected in surveys throughout the country with
other community health faculty; though the data was not perfectly
accurate, it delineated the areas of the Himalayas with the highest
health needs, greatest poverty, and least development. This data later
guided our focus areas for H.E.L.P. outreach.

Tim, who had experience with environmental impact studies
related to the hydropower project, taught university students and
learned from the country experts about water management and
landslide problems. Unpublished data and locally known information
about pesticide use, water contamination problems, and locally
available resources enabled the environmental branch of H.E.L.P. to
build an effective cooperative network with others. Living in areas
where environment was being impacted by modern development,
often in a negative fashion, allowed us to fashion cheap, simple
approaches to cleanliness and safe water supplies. Based on data the
environmental students collected from water supplies, the medical
students met with a community group and learned how to facilitate
formation of a community water group, teach chlorination of water
for purification, and work together with them to achieve safe water.
Alongside these projects, we observed successes and failures of many
INGOs and NGOs, and we learned from others how to make H.E.L.P.
community work more successful.

During these two years as academicians, we had the privilege of
studying the approach of other groups to the problems of illiteracy,
economic disparity, environmental health issues, and preventive health.
Not only was it an incredible privilege to work with brilliant national

colleagues, but we also both grew further in our understanding of the development world, the Nepali government health system, and local community issues, seeing these problems through the eyes of others who were trying to help solve them. While teaching classes, doing village health surveys, and drinking tea, we learned more than all the public health courses or degree plans could have taught us. Pouring over these problems of poverty with colleagues working with NGOs, INGOs, the university, and the medical school, we learned how we could work together with others who, though they had a different faith, also sought to help their own people develop.

Working with and under the direction of national colleagues engrained further my realization that this part of the world was producing its own doctors and did not need more physicians. Instead, we needed to work with them to effect sustainable change in their communities.

Wholistic Christian Community Development

These experiences and hundreds more, emphasized to us that for a wholistic, Christian community development program to succeed, it must address literacy, agriculture, animal health, sanitation, environmental issues, income generation, and human health— equally. For personal health, it became obvious that curative

> For a wholistic, sustainable, Christian community development to succeed in bringing physical and spiritual change it must include literacy, agriculture, animal husbandry, income generation, sanitation, environmental improvement, and health, bringing change through Christ to the hearts and minds, removing the fatalistic "ke garne" attitude.

medicine was truly hopeless; treatment of root problems and early intervention before disease progression saves lives and utilizes financial resources more wisely. Tim recognized that the only way H.E.L.P. programs could improve environmental health and prevent further destruction of God's creation was by addressing agriculture, water, and sanitation needs in a wholistic fashion. The method of teaching must be interactive, culturally appropriate, technologically simple, and sustainable, based on a trainer-of-trainers method, so that those accustomed to learning by doing could practice as they learned. Emphasis must be on prevention, rather than cure, to both save resources and impact the root problems.

Though we'd had a vision (which was truly a divine inspiration) in 1997 for what H.E.L.P. would become, we needed to know the particulars of how to develop a sustainable, community-based approach in the culture of the Himalayan region. God miraculously provided us multiple opportunities through our professions and friendships to lead us along that path. God promises that if we trust in him with all our heart as we make our plans, He will direct our paths (Proverbs 3:5). His direction for us came in helping us to see the needs and understand how others with a different worldview were trying to solve those needs. In addition, the positions in which He placed us to work with and under the supervision of national colleagues deeply affected the administrative design of H.E.L.P. Rather than take the role as directors, we learned to see the role of those we served as co-laborers. To this day, the thousands of individuals who benefit from H.E.L.P.'s training programs do not know that we founded the mission agency, or that foreigners are involved in the outreach. This proves to be valuable because individuals do not come expecting handouts, but instead, practical knowledge and experience to change their lives.

Biblical Principles:

1. *To be effective Disciples of Christ, we must have His attitude of humility.* As highly trained professionals from the United States, we frequently think of ourselves as more knowledgeable than those

from the less-developed world. Yet, an attitude of humility helps us to learn from our peers as we use the talents and gifts God has given us to bring the gospel and true development. Christians in cross-cultural service must acknowledge their national colleagues' expertise as well. A spirit of humility, like that of Christ, enables us to work as co-laborers, thereby accomplishing much more than we can with a more dictatorial leadership model.

"Do nothing out of selfish ambition or vain conceit. Rather, in humility value others above yourselves . . . . Have the same mindset as Christ Jesus: who made himself nothing by taking the very nature of a servant . . . and humbled himself by becoming obedient to death." Philippians 2:3-8

2. The initial plans we made in starting H.E.L.P. were not fully developed, *but as we sought to be living sacrifices (Romans 12:1,2), and trusted in the Lord, He brought opportunities and people, directing our paths and truly making them straight in the way that He knew was best to accomplish His purposes.*

"Commit to the Lord whatever you do, and your plans will succeed." Proverbs 16:3

"Trust in the Lord with all your heart and lean not on your own understanding; in all your ways acknowledge him, and he will make your paths straight." Proverbs 3:5,6

Figure 1. Life in Shangri-La

Shangri-La represents a particular area in the Himalayas still closed to the gospel, where persecution is intense. Because of the sensitive nature of both gospel and development work, this term is used to describe the area to protect those serving Christ there today.

1.1 Yak-herder in Shangri-la near our home.

1.2 Tibetan Buddhist prayer flags—devout Buddhists believe their prayers are sent heavenward when written on these flags.

1.3 A fortress in Shangri-La.

1.4 Curious Buddhist monks who later visited and stayed with us.

1.5 Tim hiking in the Himalayas.

1.6 Young Buddhist monks in a nearby monastery.

Life in Shangri-La

Figure 2. Our friends in the village

2.1   Kristen, Aaron, and Austin helping neighbors husk corn. They are sitting in the yard between our mud house and Hajur-Ama's house.

2.2   Hajur-Ama, grandmother, the matriarch of the village, and our educational guide to life in rural Nepal.

2.3   Austin, a toddler, leaning on the wall of our mud home; this is where he nearly died from an accidental overdose, croup, a dog bite, and innumerable environmental hazards.

2.4   Neighbor ladies and children in our village, congregating to visit with us.

2.5   Tim with Pasang, a co-worker overseeing the reforestation at the hydropower project site, having tea in Pasang's home.

Our friends in the village

Figure 3. Family Activities

3.1   Ackerman family in the town of H.E.L.P. headquarters in 2003.

3.2   Aaron and Austin growing up in a more "modern" town.

3.3   Home school learning from a local potter.

3.4   Kristen's 11th birthday party with Kayla and some of the girls from Jyoti Niwas.

3.5   Tim and the children proudly showing their vegetable produce from the backyard garden.

3.6   Family trekking in the Langtang area in an attempt at a relaxing vacation.

Family Activities

Figure 4. Literacy Classes and Training

4.1 H.E.L.P. literacy staff Mr. Shrestha with new literacy facilitators, training how to use teaching materials and distributing books they will carry to their villages for classes.

4.2 Literacy class in a remote mountain village in Nepal; students read their books by lamplight and candle as there is no electricity, as in most of rural Nepal.

4.3 Pasang, a traditional birth assistant (TBA) in village near the Tibetan border, teaching literacy students about safe motherhood and healthy maternity care. She learned to read and write, as well as received her training as a TBA from H.E.L.P.

4.4 Proud student with her baby, holding her literacy book written and published by H.E.L.P.

4.5 Literacy/non-formal education class held in a church. Students are having fun learning how to read, write, and perform simple math.

4.6. Literacy facilitators holding candles representing Christ, the light of the world, and literacy, the light of the mind, dedicating themselves to the service of God and their communities.

4.7. Student in a H.E.L.P. literacy class in a remote village, reading and writing the Nepali alphabet on the blackboard; H.E.L.P. provides the teacher, materials, blackboard, and kerosene lantern.

Literacy Classes and Training

Figure 5. Health Training

5.1   Nepali farmer standing by the outhouse he learned why and how to build through H.E.L.P., but dug himself.

5.2   H.E.L.P. health staff crossing a dilapidated suspension bridge going to a village for a training class.

5.3   H.E.L.P. health staff, teaching about health, treating illness, and praying for healing in a village church.

5.4   Christian women learning how to use a fetoscope to listen to heart sounds of the unborn baby at a Traditional Birth Assistant (TBA) training.

5.5   Lani examining children in a village as she teaches a H.E.L.P. health staff, Miss Tamang, who is a Certified Medical Assistant.

5.6   Committed Christian young people at a Village Health Worker (VHW) training learn about the causes of fever and how to read a thermometer.

5.7   Mrs. Magar, H.E.L.P. nurse midwife, teaches Christian leaders at a Village Health Worker training how to make a bamboo frame for a pit-latrine (outhouse) at a H.E.L.P. health training. Training is practical: see one, build one, teach one.

5.8   H.E.L.P. Health staff Mr. Shah performs tests for water contamination to visibly demonstrate to the village the contamination of local water supplies, and then to demonstrate ways to prevent the impurities.

Health Training

Figure 6. Agriculture Training

6.1   Interested farmers learn how to do simple soil testing and find ways of improving their agriculture production at a Farmer's training.

6.2   Christian farmer group leader who learned organic farming method and composting from H.E.L.P. stands in his field next to his non-Christian brother's field where old techniques were used, demonstrating the benefit of effective microorganism and pesticide-free farming.

6.3   H.E.L.P. agriculture staff, Mr. Prajapati, and group representatives cross a flooded stream to reach the community where they will do follow-up training in vegetable farming and composting.

6.4.   Young Christian couple, subsistence farmers, learn hands-on pesticide free farming at a H.E.L.P. model farm. They receive discipleship spiritually and practically in farming.

6.5   Bim, one of thousands of farmer's transformed by the agriculture program. At a H.E.L.P. farmer training he learned how to produce more crops, and build a smokeless stove. As one of the poorest in his village, group representatives gave him the recipe and mold to make charcoal "briquettes" to replace firewood and save forests and time gathering wood. Now this helps his community while providing his family an income.

6.6   Farmers reading the quarterly "Vineyard" magazine which shares new agriculture techniques, healthy recipes, methods for preserving vegetables, and testimonies of farmers who have followed Christ. This is the first widely circulated farmer's newsletter in simple Nepali, in a country of predominately subsistence farmers.

Agriculture Training

Figure 7. Animal Husbandry/Veterinary Training

7.1   Trainees constructing a pen for holding water buffalo and cows to vaccinate at a H.E.L.P. animal husbandry training program.

7.2   H.E.L.P. traditional birth assistant, Tika, benefited from veterinary training, as well, and teaches others how to make a smokeless stove after learning how to make one in her own home. The trainer of trainers philosophy—See one—do one—teach one plus integration of all departments of training are key in community development.

7.3   Goats lick mineral blocks their owner learned to make at a H.E.L.P. animal husbandry training.

7.4   Young man stands by his goat and newly constructed pen, now preventing hoof rot, providing cover, and producing more income for his family.

7.5   Local farmer with her new chicken farm H.E.L.P. not only assisted her in starting, but continued to provide follow up training to ensure healthy livestock and good economic return.

7.6   Animal husbandry H.E.L.P. staff, Mr. Acharya, Mr. Prajapati, and Mr. Raju on their way to a village for follow-up and training in agriculture and animal husbandry.

Animal Husbandry/Veterinary Training

Figure 8. Jyoti Niwas, "House of Light"

8.1   Children learning practical farming techniques as they plant crops for their own consumption in fields by their home.

8.2   Children walking in line from school.

8.3   New orphan baby, Samuel, after arrival and recovery from leg fracture.

8.4   Girls of Jyoti Niwas, rescued from lives of poverty and previously at risk for prostitution, performing traditional Nepali dance at a program.

8.5   Jyoti Niwas children a year after home opens, prior to construction of their home. (in a small rented facility)

8.6   Jyoti Niwas children enjoying a picnic on the roof.

Jyoti Niwas, "House of Light"

Figure 9. God's Love in Action

9.1 Traditional birth assistants learning how to palpate the mother's belly. If the baby is lying across (transverse lie) she will often accompany the mother to a city where there is an operative facility near the time of her delivery, to prevent the death of both mother and baby.

9.2 Mr. Prajapati, head agriculturalist, does follow-up field surveys in the villages on use of pesticides and water contamination. Follow-up and practical research are key in improving our agriculture program.

9.3 Farmer's folk festival with a lively farmer's group teaching a song about God's blessing and their new techniques, using traditional methods of song and dance. Farmers groups from all over Nepal send representatives to compete and have a time of celebration.

9.4 Tim, with Mrs. Bajracharya, H.E.L.P. national director, and Mr. Prajapati, after village visits and a celebration of thanks from local leaders.

9.5 Mr. Shah, health director for HELP, teaching new Village Health Workers how to clean and bandage wounds.

9.6 EM Effective Microorganism, a blend of beneficial microorganisms used in composting and organic farming. This is a sustainable technology for improving farming methods while decreasing pesticide use and has been highly successful in our farmer's training programs.

Figure 10. Lives changed

10.1 Rai family—one of thousands transformed from poverty to spiritual and physical wholeness through H.E.L.P. Christian community development. At the time of this photo they had a poultry farm, vermiculture, and large garden on a piece of rented land, and were not only able to feed their family well, but send their children to a good school. Mr. Rai was recognized by the local government as the most outstanding farmer of the year!

10.2 Group Representative Pastor Kedar, with one of numerous church congregations started through local community development efforts of H.E.L.P.

10.3 Literacy class of predominately Hindu ladies who crushed rock to earn $1 a day, and used their own money to build a small shelter where the literacy facilitator (a local follower of Christ) could teach them non-formal education classes.

10.4 One of many new groups of TBA's—ladies who spend their own time to come to H.E.L.P.'s trainings so they can save mothers and babies in their communities, as they share love and the good news of Christ.

10.5 Pastor and his wife who saw no response to the gospel, until they demonstrated the love of Christ by not only improving their own production of tomatoes through H.E.L.P.'s agriculture program training, but teaching their neighbors how to do so.

10.6 Older couple who had suffered from lung disease from wood smoke, in their kitchen with a newly built smokeless stove. They learned to build it through a H.E.L.P. program organized by the local church.

Lives changed

Book Two

Chapter 5

Christian Community Development Defined

In the developing world, *community development* commonly refers to a set of values and practices that helps a given community overcome poverty and disadvantage through a grassroots, wholistic approach, enabling the people in that community to live healthy, productive lives. *Sustainable* development in this context refers to development which can be sustained, or continued, through local resources without ongoing need for outside funding and expertise.

Most community development programs in the developing world include informal education or literacy in the local language, food production (agriculture, animals), improved farming, animal husbandry, income generation, preventive and basic curative health, sanitation and improved housing, economic development, environmental improvement (prevention of deforestation, erosion, landslides), and a sense of cooperation between families. In establishing H.E.L.P., we interpreted community development in the perspective of the cultures of the people in the Himalayan region and chose departments to represent the needs of those areas. We chose the following branches: literacy (informal education including reading, writing, basic math and business skills in the local language), agriculture, animal husbandry, income generation (often linked to agriculture and animal husbandry), health, environment and sanitation, and compassionate care (orphaned, underprivileged, and abandoned children; abandoned elderly).

A New Kind of Community Development

Christian community development, particularly in the two-thirds world,[34] is a relatively new concept, and therefore one for which few definitions or examples exist. We believe Christian community

> Christian community development is not simply Christian people involved in secular community development, nor is it only development done in the love of Christ. It is much, much more.

development must be Christ-centered and administered through His vehicle to reach the world, the church. Many outstanding relief and development organizations were started or are directed by Christians, but the primary objective is often meeting human needs. The Bible calls us to "do good and share with others" (Hebrews 13:16) as well as care for the poor, but assistance is focused first on the "household of faith" and is *always* hand in hand with attention to spiritual needs and the spread of the gospel. Jesus clearly demonstrated compassion for mankind's human needs, but always in light of mankind's spiritual needs, with the ultimate focus on our eternal destiny.

> *What good is it for someone to gain the whole world, yet forfeit their soul?* Mark 8:36

The definition and description of Christian community development from the original H.E.L.P. documents was built entirely on study of the Scripture, the direction and leading of the Holy Spirit, and the experiences God had given us within various ethnic communities in the United States and abroad. More than community development done by Christians for relief of physical deprivation and poverty in the name of Jesus, Christian community development is

---

[34] *Two-thirds world* is another term for the third world, emphasizing that two-thirds of the world's population is in this category.

that which models a Biblical approach with Biblical goals of spiritual discipleship, as well.

Luke the physician, in the book of Acts, describes the early community of Christians as one that shared everything—expertise, work, finances, land—and cared for its own. The most powerful time of church evangelism occurred during a time when Christians cared for one another and reached out in love to

> In Christian community development, values and practices taught through the believing church to the community enable and empower the community to develop wholistically and to live healthy and productive lives in this physical world, as well as in preparation for the life beyond.

their communities. Despite cultural persecution, God brought signs and wonders, and "numbers were added daily" (Acts 16:5). In the first-century church, as in many churches among recently reached or unreached people groups today, following Christ often meant the loss of family, social status, property, and employment. Christians worked together to provide for those who suffered, sharing their possessions. There were no handouts, as Paul later wrote: "If a man does not work, he should not eat" (2 Thessalonians 3:10). Church communities gave out of their poverty to brothers and sisters in times of famine or hardship. Some of these communities were composed of Jewish converts, but in both Acts and in the epistles, we see new communities of believers who, like those we were called to serve in the Himalayas, came out of a polytheistic world view and religion. Paul wrote that we are called to help all those in need but "especially to those who belong to the family of believers" (Galatians 6:10). Christian community development, then, seeks initially to provide for the physical needs of the brothers and sisters within the church.

While we first seek to provide skills to empower believers in Christ, we also teach believers to care for one another's needs and the needs of their families. John repeatedly tells us they will "know that you are my disciples, if you love one another" (John 13:35). When the Christian community shares care and concern for a young Christian's family, that believer's testimony becomes a powerful witness to unbelievers in a world where birth, status, and family caste regulates relationships.

The author of Hebrews prays, "May the God of peace . . . equip you with everything good for doing his will" (Hebrews 13:20-21). Though only Christ equips us with His spirit and power, Christian community development is a means for the church to equip young believers with skills for living healthy, productive lives. It can even provide economic freedom for those who lose their livelihood when they follow Christ. In the developing world, this equipping includes life skills such as:

1. How to read, write, perform basic math, and understand basic health and sanitation through non-formal education in the local language.
2. How to grow crops by utilizing even limited land wisely to produce the most nutritious food possible without damaging God's creation. Surplus crops can be sold for income and living expenses.
3. How to raise healthy livestock for food and income.
4. How to have access to clean water and safe food, and how to avoid simple diseases that can result in early death and disability.
5. How to generate income to care for themselves, enabling them to give back to God and care for the poor and vulnerable of their own community.

Paul urged Timothy to teach the things he was taught "to reliable people who will also be qualified to teach others also" (II Timothy

2:2). Christian community development must also include Christian discipleship. While learning how to grow better crops, participants also receive spiritual food in life skills and scripture. As they learn how to read and write from a Christian brother or sister, they are discipled in their spiritual

> Christian community development is the discipleship process of equipping and empowering young believers so that they can care for themselves and their families as well as develop their own communities. It is teaching believers to love God first, and then love their neighbors as themselves.

life, as well. As they receive health training, medical treatment, or have their baby delivered by a Christian brother or sister, they are also being equipped and discipled. Each one learns, and then teaches others. Each step of training is passed on to others in a discipleship chain. Because Christian community development addresses spiritual as well as physical development, it must take place through the church and must be led by dedicated followers of Christ. Unbelievers will witness the unity that results from the discipleship process. Through this unity and love for one another, Christians also demonstrate Christ's love for the world and prove the reality of their faith in the living God.

Christian community development teaches reliable men and women skills of literacy, agriculture, animal husbandry, health, sanitation, and income generation, alongside spiritual skills that they, in turn, teach others. It *also enables* national Christians to sustain themselves physically and spiritually, without dependence on outside resources, in a mutually beneficial and sustainable means. This creates unity between brothers and sisters in the Lord, and allows compassionate ministry to flow directly from the local church to the local community.

The Great Commission (Matthew 28:19-20) is the mandate to "go and make disciples of all nations." But in many areas of the world, particularly those yet to receive the gospel, Christianity may be rejected based on presuppositions that it is a foreign religion. Historically, political objectives have been mixed with so-called missionary work, breeding distrust. Equally destructive, nominal Christianity may be tolerated and amalgamated into the myriad of gods already accepted. Christian community development is the means by which we see the gospel advanced and the church growing as in the book of Acts, as those outside the church witness the amazing selflessness, love, and unity of believers.

> *Simply preaching Jesus is Lord means nothing to a society steeped in idolatry—He is just another god to add to the mantle. To a community which has never experienced true compassion and neighborly love, seeing love in action from a believer is the most powerful and sustainable witness of all.*

Old Testament Jewish laws of cleanliness, as well as recorded examples of sin followed by physical disease, illustrate the close connection between spiritual and physical health. Jesus's own ministry, likewise, exemplifies the marriage of physical and spiritual needs. At the feeding of the 5,000 men (plus women and children), he "had compassion" for the sick, and though the disciples told him to send the people away after teaching them all day, He also had compassion for their hunger, and instead multiplied a young boy's loaves and fish to meet their physical and spiritual needs together. (Matthew 14: 14-21; Mark 6:34-44). Luke even specifically mentions in his account that on the day of this miracle "He (Jesus) welcomed them and spoke to them about the kingdom of God, and healed those who needed healing." (Luke 9:11). On one occasion of healing a blind man (John 9:1-38), after the healed man is accused by the hypocritical Pharisees, Jesus comes to him, and explains that He is the Messiah. The man responds, "Lord, I believe" (John 9:38) and worshipped Him. Virtually all physical healings are linked with preaching God's kingdom and the salvation of sinners. Jesus simply did not separate physical and spiritual healing.

In addition, Jesus replied to the question of which is the greatest commandment, "'Love the Lord your God with all your heart, and with all your soul and with all your mind.' This is the first and greatest commandment. And the second is like it: 'love your neighbor as yourself'" (Matthew 22:37-39).

The church should be the *avenue* of development and learning. When an educated young man spends two hours daily teaching his neighbor how to read and write, he is *loving his neighbor*. When a believer equipped as a traditional birth assistant or village community health worker saves the life or limb of an unbelieving neighbor, for no pay or benefit to herself, she is *loving her neighbor*. When a pastor, trained in better ways to raise goats or grow

> **Herein lays the secret to the success of Christian community development in the effective, culturally appropriate and sustainable spread of the gospel as modeled in the Scripture. When a community of believers, equipped with appropriate skills and full of the Holy Spirit, love their neighbors as themselves, they effectively demonstrate the love of God in Christ and win a hearing for the good news of salvation through Jesus.**

crops, teaches his neighbors how they can have a better livelihood, his concern for his friends physical needs wins the right to share the Way, Truth, and Life. If Christians, because of their love for Christ and their neighbors, take the lead in developing their own communities, they win a hearing for the truth of the gospel. Christian community development is also the process by which Christians (in our case, first-generation) receive training, and in turn train others of their community, becoming leaders in all areas of life. It is love in action, validating the truth of the God of the gospel.

Christian community development is a means of empowering young Christians to effectively witness their real faith in a living God by loving their neighbors as themselves, as they develop their communities and improve the physical and spiritual health of their neighbors, as they themselves have been equipped. It is a Biblical, practical means to give the good news of the gospel to the nations. The story of the grassroots movement started by H.E.L.P. is an example of how the Holy Spirit is miraculously working in a first-generation church, empowering nationals to grow in their faith and change the world, one community at a time. This is the rest of the story as it is unfolding today.

Biblical Principles

1. *The key to Christian community development is for believers in Christ to first love the Lord with all their heart, and then love their neighbors.* "'Love the Lord your God with all your heart, and with all your soul and with all your mind.' This is the first and greatest commandment. And the second is like it: 'love your neighbor as yourself'" (Matthew 22:37-39). If we simply try to create an environment to "do good" separate from a love for the Lord, not only will individuals quickly lose their enthusiasm and zeal, but they will only do those acts of service which benefit themselves or bring recognition. In contrast, those who serve out of a love for the Lord, look to Him for their recognition (Matthew 6:1) True love of Christ is not just in word, but in action (I John 3:18).

2. *Demonstrating the love of Christ by loving one another first, and then loving others, was key in the growth of the early church, as it is in a first-generation church, or any church, today.* Galatians 6:10 emphasizes that our first responsibility is to the "household of faith," and then to the rest of the world. Christian community

98

development focuses first on believers, but then through those believers impacts the world.

3. In the ministry of Jesus, as well as in the early church, Christ and his disciples recognized both spiritual and physical needs. We too, must recognize and meet both types of need, while not excluding the more important needs of the soul. Jesus ministered to the body and spirit. Missions focused solely on evangelism or solely on social ministries are both incorrect—Jesus did not only heal or feed the crowds, he gave them the good news of eternal life. However, as he preached, he also met their physical needs. We must do the same. James emphasizes faith with works: "If one of you says to them, 'Go in peace; keep warm and well fed,' but does nothing about their physical needs, what good is it? In the same way, faith by itself, if it is not accompanied by action, is dead." James 2:16-17

Chapter 6

Leadership Development

Himalayan Conditions

To understand our work as it unfolded in God's plan, one must appreciate the conditions in which H.E.L.P. operates. The Himalayan region ranges from sea level (the *terai* area of Nepal) to the highest mountain in the world, Mount Everest. In Nepal, home to H.E.L.P.'s headquarters, there are approximately twenty-nine million people and over 340 people groups (*ethnos*), each with its own language and culture. The dominant language is Nepali. The surrounding countries are home to various ethnic groups, many similar to those living in Nepal. Traditionally, most people living in the Himalayas have followed Hinduism or Tibetan Buddhism. Both of these religions believe in a multitude of gods, reincarnation, and *karma* (fate). These beliefs deeply affect people's lives. In addition to frequent religious holidays and *pujas* (ceremonies), fatalism permeates the pervading worldview. Poverty, illness, and other woes are often believed to result from sins committed in a previous life. A strict caste system dictates to whom one may talk, eat, socialize, or marry. An understanding of caste relations and prejudices is critical to working in this part of the world. While leaders in higher education and government officials do their best through policy changes and laws to address some of these issues, the ideas are deeply ingrained in the culture, especially among those living in rural areas.

Life expectancy is short and women frequently die in childbirth. Outside the big cities, hospital and other medical facilities are sparse and unaffordable for many. Though medical schools and nursing programs are now producing many graduates, infrastructure and supplies for these professionals are often lacking. As in many developing countries, some of the best students leave their country seeking better opportunities. Undeveloped areas offer little or nothing to attract and retain more highly educated young people. Electricity and running water tend to be luxuries only the rich can afford. Though motorized vehicles are available in more urban areas, many areas are only accessible by foot. Toilets and outhouses are uncommon in rural areas; most communities do not recognize the need for them. Survival is precarious, with many infants succumbing to simple diseases before a month of age, and even more by age five. In rural areas, malnutrition rates among young children approach 70 percent. Though national literacy and education rates are slowly improving, poor and rural communities have been minimally impacted by the millions of aid dollars poured into these areas.

Nepal, as well as surrounding areas of the Himalayas, is near the bottom of the world in income and development. Most people are subsistence farmers, with production on their worn-out land inadequate to even feed the family for a full year. Animal husbandry and agriculture production are some of the only reliable means for income generation, but most villagers do not have the training or understanding to make a living in this way. Jobs in the city often do not materialize, and those who leave their family and community also lose the social support so integral in the culture. Those who seek employment in the city often find nothing but greater hardships, compounding the economic problems of the family they leave in the village. In recent years, a huge migration of the young workforce to other countries, often after incurring loans to pay their travel costs, is resulting in division of families and destitution of those left behind. When coupled with displacement, poverty often results in prostitution, alcoholism, abandoned elderly and children, and other societal problems.

H.E.L.P. Programs Develop

Working with women on a daily basis, I grew frustrated by the way it seemed their minds had literally become dulled and listless. The combination of hopelessness, oppression, malnutrition, and a general belief that they were trapped in a fatalistic situation often did not change, despite my best efforts. Doctors, nurses, and public health experts working in the developing world know that the key to changing women's ability to care for their children, and even the infant mortality rate,[35] is maternal literacy. Literate, educated women play a critical role in determining the success of their children regardless of the culture, but this is particularly true in developing nations. Early on, we knew that to make a difference in the health of communities, literacy must be the foundation of a program; we decided that the first H.E.L.P. trainings must focus on non-formal education.[36]

---

[35] Infant mortality rate is the ratio of the number of deaths in the first year of life to the number of live births in the same population the same time. The basic ability of the mother to read and write in her language (literacy) is linked statistically with her child's survival.

[36] *Non-formal education* refers to literacy classes for older children or adult learners. Classes incorporate social, health, basic mathematics, and business ideals in addition to reading and writing.

Starting with Literacy

The first outreach of H.E.L.P. began shortly after we returned to Nepal in 1999. Kristen and Aaron briefly attended a local school, where they met two other children who were Christians. (chapter 4) We became friends with their parents and shared our desire to start a literacy class as the first building block of our program. Their mother, Mrs. Bajracharya[37], a highly-educated and vivacious Christian with experience in community and educational work, wanted to demonstrate Christ's love in a practical way to some of her friends. She offered to begin our first literacy class in her home, teaching local women who had never had the opportunity to attend school. A few months later, a young pastor and his wife, the Badals, who had just returned home after completing seminary in India (sponsored by a US denomination), expressed excitement and desire to reach out by offering a literacy class to their Hindu friends as well as women in their church.

"My daughter does not need to be literate; she will just be married and bear children."

This was the attitude of some of the men, but not all. Many forward-thinking leaders, including Christian leaders, were beginning to recognize the importance of literacy for the development of their country. In rural areas and even many larger cities, literacy rates were low for men *and* women. Government-sponsored schools were opening, but the average farmer with six children could only afford to

---

[37] As mentioned earlier, only last names (and sometimes pseudonyms) are given as many of these individuals work in sensitive areas, and these names are "caste" based, showing the variety of people groups and castes involved in the ministry of H.E.L.P.

send his sons to school. Civil unrest from the Maoist insurgency[38] drove away teachers in some areas and lack of payment discouraged others. Non-formal education classes taught by the government and other non-governmental organizations (NGOs) helped in some districts, but many programs were mismanaged, as we had witnessed in the village, classes were often cancelled, and teachers came only for payday. Few people actually benefited. When our first classes were highly successful—testimonies, tears of joy, and transformed lives—we were again convinced that literacy and non-formal education must be the backbone of development and the foundation of the entire H.E.L.P. program.

> **Cross-training departments and the trainer-of-trainers method became central to H.E.L.P.'s development.**

Several months after the first literacy classes started, we met an enthusiastic young Christian from southern Nepal. We were searching for a Certified Medical Assistant (CMA) to begin development of our health department. In the rural communities, a CMA, having completed tenth grade and fifteen months of medical training, functions as a village doctor. Frequently, the CMA owns a pharmacy shop and can legally examine patients and dispense medications. When we interviewed Mr. Shah, he shared his vision to spread the gospel *through* his medical work. We were impressed with his commitment, even at only twenty years of age. Unfortunately though, due to problems with his licensure exam, he could not begin working in health immediately. Since we had no programs other than literacy, we asked him to start teaching a new H.E.L.P. literacy class,

---

[38] Maoist insurgency or civil war was a conflict between Nepali Maoist Communists and government forces primarily lasting from 1996-2006, though there was fighting before and after, which caused significant death and suffering.

requested by another group of local women. As Nepali was his second language (his first was Maithili), we were concerned with his mastery of proper Nepali. Using the trainer-of-trainers method, which includes observing other teachers and receiving feedback on teaching, Mr. Shah blossomed into a natural leader. Later, each department would spend time with the other, learning that all were important, just as in Christ's body each member must use his or her gifts to complete the task of evangelism and promote God's kingdom. In addition, by spending his first nine months teaching illiterate women, he became burdened with the plight of women in his country, understood their health needs better, and recognized the critical role of literacy in health of the community. This knowledge assisted him as he became the director and developer of the health department for the next twelve years.

Health Ministry Begins

After successfully receiving his credentials, Mr. Shah began meeting with church leaders in the district[39] and surrounding areas to identify their community needs. We started offering regular medical outreaches in underserved areas to teach health and to provide free care in the churches. Often these became times for diagnosis and treatment, as well as healing services. Most importantly, they broke down barriers in the community so that those from other religions recognized they would not be "cursed" by crossing the threshold of a home or building used as a Christian church. In addition, the Christians offering care and concern established a reputation of compassion and love as demonstrated by our Savior. Though our health focus changed dramatically in later years, with much more emphasis on prevention

---

[39] Districts are much like states—areas of government in Nepal. There are fourteen administrative zones and seventy-five districts.

and public health, initially we provided both curative and preventive care. In areas with few local medications, we brought subsidized medications and performed examinations while teaching locals about simple treatable diseases and sanitation. Believers reported that the host churches experienced an explosion of new followers of Christ and community unity.

After a few overwhelming "camps" with more patients than we could possibly examine in a few hours, Mr. Shah and I discussed our need to develop a training program for village health workers (VHWs). Rather than the common practice of NGOs and government trainers paying people to attend training and classroom lecture-based learning, we determined to train young believers chosen by their community or church without pay, using the trainer-of-trainers model with a hands-on focus. In this way, the Christians could take the medical knowledge we taught them and teach others also, as they shared the good news of Christ. It was the only way we could possibly meet the insurmountable needs of poverty-stricken communities while sharing the good news of the gospel. In addition, we recognized that medical outreaches were impractical. H.E.L.P. did not have enough full-time medical staff to visit more than a few areas, and on our limited budget, we would be unable to help other communities if we spent all of our money on medicine, clinics, and staff. Though government facilities existed on the maps, a lack of budget, medicines, and personnel kept curative care difficult to access. Many people had no basic care, and no trust in "modern" medicine when it was available at a government facility. A focus on training local Christian leaders to be the first line of defense in teaching their neighbors about hygiene, sanitation, and simple treatments of common ailments made sense. With education, zeal, follow-up, and a love for their people and Christ, these volunteer VHWs (referred to by some as community health evangelists) could prevent or avert life-threatening illnesses. Our small organization could not financially support services available through government health posts or other, better-funded non-government organizations. In areas where care was available, therefore, we determined to build relationships and work together in our common goals of health promotion, prevention, and treatment. These foundational principles allowed a rapid expansion, a spirit of cooperation rather than competition with other non-faith-based groups, and wiser use of our limited resources.

Mother-Baby Care

After a year spent learning more about medical needs and increasing our familiarity with the overwhelming maternal and infant mortality rates in the Himalayas, we recognized the need for a focus on obstetrical and infant care. In much of the developing world, traditional birth assistants (TBAs) or relatives perform most deliveries; any pre-natal care that exists is performed by the same minimally trained, but dedicated, women. In Nepal and surrounding areas, the mother-in-law frequently supervises the birth of a baby. She often has the reputation of being oppressive to her daughter-in-law; her level of attentiveness to the young woman in labor can range from excellent to minimal. Even with best intentions, these women often do not know basic hygiene and follow customs requiring the "unclean" delivery to occur in an "unclean" animal stall. Some castes require the woman to deliver alone, with no assistance. All of these barriers to care make the TBA, a local married woman trained in critical preventive care and education, an important link for both the village woman without access to care and the village woman with access but no trust in the local clinic or hospital. For women with geographic access to care but whose families are afraid of more modern practices, the TBA plays a necessary role in building trust by accompanying a village mother to the clinic.

In traditional cultures, women often do not feel comfortable talking to men about their medical problems. Our CMA was young and inexperienced; we needed a committed Christian nurse midwife to lead and develop our program for TBAs and maternal and child health workers. As before, we prayed and asked the Lord to send the right person. Various friends recommended some ladies, but when we met Mrs. Magar, she was clearly the one God chose for this position. Mrs. Magar had graduated from nursing school as a nurse midwife a few years before, and was serving with her husband in church ministry and evangelism. She had been trained by Campus Crusade for Christ, but had no means of financial support. In addition, she wanted to use her skills in midwifery to lead her people to Christ and improve the lives and safety of women delivering babies. She joined with Mr. Shah and started developing our village program to train Christian women as TBAs, beginning with their education in nutrition, hygiene, and healthy delivery practices.

Less than a year later, through the recommendation of a trusted pastor friend, a newly graduated young CMA joined the health team. When we interviewed Miss Tamang for the position, we were excited to realize she was from the caste of an unreached Tibetan Buddhist people group for whom we had been praying for opportunity to impact. The Bible had not yet been completely translated into her language, and there were few believers; most of these Eastern Tamang mountain people had never heard the name of Jesus. Again, God had brought another strong, young Christian with a desire to share her faith and serve her people. When I asked her why she wanted to work with H.E.L.P., she tearfully told the story of her aunt, who died in childbirth from a simple retained placenta,[40] a common but easily treatable cause of maternal death in the developing world. After her aunt's death, Miss Tamang decided to become a CMA in order to minister to her own people and to other villagers in rural areas who had no knowledge of safe delivery practices. Prior to her training she also had left Buddhism to follow Christ. Amazingly, God was bringing quality representatives from many language and people groups and castes; the unity He would demonstrate to a world directed by prejudice based on birth and family tribes became a powerful witness to the unity of the church. These national H.E.L.P. missionaries[41] demonstrated that high-caste Brahmins could eat, work, and fellowship with Dalits, Tharus, and Tamangs[42] as they worked together to build their communities into better places to live.

Literacy Expands

While the health and literacy teams were beginning to build relationships with groups of believers in surrounding areas, we recognized the need for a full-time literacy coordinator. After much prayer, God led us to Mr. Shrestha, a young man with a vision to start churches and disciple believers through literacy. He recognized that Christians leading in development could break down caste and

---

[40] The placenta, or afterbirth, sometimes does not spontaneously deliver after the birth of the baby. This prevents contraction of the uterus, and can lead to infection, bleeding, and death if no intervention is done.

[41] National missionary is a term referring to a person living in his own country, who actively shares his faith in Christ with his own people or with other ethnic groups who may be similar to his own tribe or caste.

[42] Brahmins are highest caste and Dalits are the lowest caste. Tamangs (Eastern and Western) and Tharus are other tribal groups. Traditionally, these groups do not associate closely with each other, but on the H.E.L.P. staff they work closely together in fellowship and service.

religious barriers, even for those who did not choose to follow Christ, giving believers an opportunity to share their faith in a practical way while helping to develop their own communities. With an evangelistic fervor, he launched a heart-felt, Spirit-anointed campaign to bring the gift of reading, writing, and basic math to those who had never had the opportunity to learn. Within five years he grew our literacy department from a handful of classes serving about 30 students each year, to one reaching 1,700 students per year in districts many miles from our headquarters. He soon recruited and trained another, younger colleague, Mr. Ramtel; together they began improving teaching methods, writing their own materials and empowering communities through literacy.

Animal Husbandry and Agriculture Work Begins

As work developed in health and literacy, economic issues continued to come to the forefront. Most people in the Himalayan region live on the edge of poverty and starvation; Nepal ranks at the bottom of the development index. Unemployment in the cities is rampant, and farmers frequently have inadequate land to provide food for their families. We knew raising livestock could provide income and improve nutrition. Even when roads were closed by landslides or civil turmoil and buses were not available, food from livestock could be eaten or sold in a local market. Shortly after we began praying for leadership in animal husbandry, we met a church leader, Mr. Acharya, with skills in raising healthy goats. Due to his aptitude for learning, and desire to serve Christ, we sent him for additional training to become a certified veterinarian technician.[43] Mr. Acharya began training farmers in methods for raising healthier, bigger goats to provide more food and more income.

When the health team shared about the need for improved methods to rid kitchens of smoke and prevent burns caused by children falling into fires, Mr. Acharya, an engineer by on-the-job training, immediately launched a *duwa rahit chulo* program. Using his own village home and church as a field test, he and his wife experimented with various designs, finding the one that best eliminated smoke and conserved wood while efficiently cooking food. He learned from others and adapted his methods, depending on the altitude of the village, available building materials, and desire for more or less heat production for the home (depending on climate). A few months later, a local pastor asked us to equip one of his promising young leaders with practical skills in animal husbandry and teaching. H.E.L.P. funded Mr. Raju to complete the two-year veterinarian technician training program. These two men—one older and one younger—began our animal husbandry and veterinary program.

Prior to beginning the animal husbandry department, we prayed for a national Christian leader with expertise in agriculture. While over 80 percent of Himalayan people earn their income through farming, the highly trained farmers who are not only book smart but actually willing to till the soil are quickly hired by government agencies or well-funded INGOs. Civil war continued in many areas of the country, shutting down most of the internationally funded development work. A Christian INGO directed by our close friends had to disband due

---

[43]   In the villages and in even larger towns, veterinary technicians practically function as veterinarians, providing immunizations and medications. This function is highly valued in a country of 29 million with fewer than 200 veterinary graduates each year.

to political instability. As we were wondering how H.E.L.P. could ever hope to assist poor farmers in their plight to grow food or produce crops using natural means with more organic methods, we received a call from our friends. Mr. Prajapati, their agriculturalist, needed a job. When we asked him why he wanted to join H.E.L.P., he replied:

"I want to share the gospel and uplift the poor farmers of Nepal, make farming more than just subsistence . . . I want to help them make farming a business."

Mr. Prajapati understood that sharing the gospel and discipling Christians *while* teaching them to grow crops more efficiently and earn a living, is Christian community development in action—just as through non-formal education, health training and animal husbandry. In addition, he recognized that unless farming became profitable enough to be an economic incentive to the youths of Nepal, the villages, families, and churches would suffer from their migration to the city or abroad.

Building a Headquarters

As work in all areas grew rapidly, we recognized the need for a training center. Ideally we did not want a building, but there was no place to hold trainings, house an office for staff and supplies, and (later) to house homeless children. We needed to have a meeting center, a place of lodging for those attending training from all over the Himalayas, and a headquarters. Until 2010, Nepal was a Hindu monarchy, and laws as well as landlord pressures affected freedom to worship or speak openly of Christian faith. Originally dubbed *Manthano*, (learning, in Greek) the building had to be secure from thieves and animals, and it needed to be surrounded by fields we could use for experimental agriculture plots during training. After Tim drew up a design for the building, a local pastor and friend, Mr. Badal (whose wife started one of the initial literacy classes), began oversight of the plans. We soon became concerned, however, as it seemed the local contractors did not have the same attention to budget and details as we did, and Mr. Badal had never undertaken such a project. In addition, there were many administrative and day-to-day duties Tim and I had no time to handle. We desperately needed a contractor, administrator, and financial expert to take the small amount of money and expand it for God's work.

At that time, our friend Mrs. Bajracharya (who began the first literacy class and whose daughters were friends with Kristen) had moved to work in the Middle East, but her husband had to return to Nepal because of health issues. He had served as the accountant at a Christian mission hospital, and knew virtually everyone in business in the area. In addition, Mr. Bajracharya had a deep personal faith in Christ and maturity as a first-generation believer.[44] Half Tibetan and half Newari, he seemed to be gifted with an ability to make every rupee go further. He could negotiate prices like no one else! God brought him to the team just in time, right as we were beginning the process of building the H.E.L.P. headquarters.

Empowering Nationals From the Start

During H.E.L.P.'s infancy, Tim and I were busy in our jobs with the university and medical school, as well as homeschooling and caring for our children. Every spare minute we spent working, praying, talking, and going to the villages with our teams and new staff. Our professional jobs were not just a way to retain visas in the country; they were a way we could personally serve the people and

---

[44] By "first-generation" this means he was the first in his family to follow Christ. His family was Tibetan Buddhist.

demonstrate loving our neighbor just as we sought to encourage our young Christian friends to love their neighbors. In fact, we helped our colleagues to see that teaching literacy, preventing and curing diseases, demonstrating new agriculture techniques, and raising more healthy animals are all part of living our lives as "living sacrifices" (Romans 12:1) as we share the gospel in word and deed. *We shared and demonstrated to them that practicing excellence in our professions, using our God-given gifts as salt and light to the world were a more powerful witness than being a full-time pastor or evangelist.*

Through regular Bible study and weekly staff meetings, Tim encouraged the national missionaries in their spiritual and professional development. These times of fellowship, sharing, planning, and prayer promoted unity, organization, purpose, and growth. In addition, we both spent hours together struggling with the health, environmental, veterinary, economic, and agriculture problems of the people, and debating how to best solve them.

The early years of H.E.L.P. were foundational in developing ideas. While building our leadership team, what initially seemed to be a hindrance—having full-time jobs and a family—was directly God's

> **Our first job in developing leadership was to ensure that the Nepali believers on our team were committed followers of Jesus *who had a vision to love the Lord their God first and love their neighbors as themselves.***

blessing. Our inability to be present at every decision, to determine the exact methods of development, and to personally meet with the local community leaders was His design; all of these issues were managed by our national colleagues from the very beginning, establishing ours as a uniquely national-governed and national-led organization. Tim's weekly leadership meetings with the staff included Bible study, prayer, sharing plans for the week, brainstorming, and assigning responsibility to each individual for various tasks. This time became foundational and the weekly leadership meetings have been held at the same time using a similar format for thirteen years. In God's perfect design, He eventually brought together eighteen full-time staff (including those of the children's home) who represented most of the major castes of the country, and who were members of a variety of denominational and non-denominational churches, speaking all the major languages of the area. This unity demonstrated both to Christians and non-Christians how individuals from different castes and backgrounds can work in unity to love the Lord and love their neighbor as they lead the way to develop communities and spread the gospel. As other believers joined the H.E.L.P. leadership team, we retained this sense of unity and single-minded purpose of bringing the gospel through community development.

Because H.E.L.P. is dedicated to *Christian* community development, we wanted to follow Christ's example of discipleship by servant leadership. The difficulty, however, was in determining how to combine the spiritual aspects of discipleship with professional excellence in development. This was, and continues to be, a challenging task. Rather than follow the existing social or governmental structure, which was in a constant state of flux, we believed God wanted us to develop communities *through* the fledgling churches. This vision resulted in our decision to work with and through the church leadership, though flawed and immature. We also worked to build relations with community and government leaders. Empowering and equipping our own staff, many of whom had significant spiritual maturity and vision before joining us, was just the beginning. Next we had to create a network where our actual trainings in each discipline were not only giving the skills to live, but also spiritual food.

> *The things you have heard me say . . . entrust to reliable men who will be qualified to teach others.* II Timothy 2:2

In developing leaders of the first-generation church, Paul recognized the discipleship principle evident in Jesus' own ministry. Jesus spent the majority of his time with twelve men, and most of the rest of his time with a limited number who, in the power of the Holy Spirit, changed the world. We focused our efforts on a handful of believers (our H.E.L.P. staff) and in turn, they continue to teach and train others both in their areas of expertise and about the life of a disciple and the Christian walk. Even in the advanced literacy class, students read about other nationals who came to Christ and the change He brought to their lives. In this way, we strive to walk as Jesus walked (I John 2:6) and teach them to do the same; we emphasize that it is a daily walk, not something restricted to one day a week or inside the walls of a church building. Just as in the New Testament church, the Christian community is the center of learning. The see one, do one, teach one philosophy of hands-on learning is built into every aspect of the H.E.L.P. program. God graciously led us to structure each department separately, yet to work together in such a way that national believers have been and are directly responsible for all avenues of learning, as they also receive teaching.

During the first four years of building H.E.L.P. we lived in the Himalayan region, interacting with our national brothers and sisters daily. When it was time to return to the United States, God made it clear to us that we, like the Apostle Paul, needed to visit our national colleagues for periodic encouragement and accountability, and yet allow them to use their own expertise to make decisions in most cases. Relinquishing most leadership roles to the nationals was only possible because we had already laid the building blocks of discipleship and leadership training. We taught and continue to teach our staff, and the learning is passed on to faithful men and women. They, in turn, teach hundreds of trainees. We follow a similar process of discipleship and mentorship with the children in our programs. This results in the reproduction of faithful disciples of Jesus and the growth of His church as they develop their own communities.

Biblical Principles

1. *In developing leadership we must follow the Apostle Paul's example and teach faithful men and women who will teach others also* (II Timothy 2:2).

   In Christian community development this includes not only scriptural principles, but principles of health, agriculture, animal husbandry, sanitation, literacy, and income generation. In addition, we must empower Christian leaders to teach others, so that discipleship continues to multiply.

2. *Christian community development is based on the premise that the church is the avenue through which God has chosen to bring His gospel.*

   Christians are to be known by our love and our unity. Demonstrating this among the leaders, between castes, and across denominations (with basic Biblical doctrines) is a testimony to the watching world. Jesus prayed in John 17:23, "May they be brought to complete unity to let the world know that you sent me and have loved them even as you have loved me." The process of Christian community development results in a spirit of unity (Romans 15:5) among believers as it draws unbelievers to Christ.

Chapter 7

How Each Branch Works

The Branches and the Vine

I am the vine, you are the branches. If you remain in me and I in you, you will bear much fruit; apart from me you can do nothing. John 15:5

John's illustration of the dependency of each branch on the vine, Christ, is much the same as the relationship between the branches, or departments, in a Christian community development program. Even in the physical realm, success depends on relationships between our national coworkers, the indigenous volunteers, and us. Because of this interdependency, it is difficult to describe the ministry of H.E.L.P by separating it into different departments; however, each branch has an imperative function in the wholistic ministry of Bible-based community development.

> To bear spiritual fruit, each branch must depend on the vine—Christ.

Two common means of administering development organizations are international non-governmental organizations (INGOs) and non-governmental organizations (NGOs). While a complete description of these entities is beyond the scope of this book, a basic understanding of these administrative means helps to understand ways of effectively running a Christian development program. An INGO includes many wealthy aid organizations and has well-paid international and national staff, full-time marketers, and well-funded programs. Large budgets provide more funding for projects, but administrative costs are high and local governments may require large bank accounts or pay-offs to work in the country. Some organizations have non-profit status and form multiple INGOs or NGOs in the countries in which they work, with large administrative budgets for staff in the United States and marketing.

NGOs can have lower administrative costs (if these are not displaced to the non-profit which manages them) and the potential to work more effectively with locals. In cases of civil conflict, NGOs may also be more accepted by rebel forces and recognized as local entities, rather than foreign invaders. However, NGOs can also misuse money administratively, and individuals may even divert funds; strict accountability between the people receiving funds and those providing funds is essential.

Currently, church denominations, Christian para-church agencies, and humanitarian organizations use both of these methods to bring funds, resources, and people into other countries. Because of our lack of money and our philosophical opposition to promoting dependency, we worked with H.E.L.P.'s national leadership team to form an NGO. Unfortunately, the formation of the NGO was delayed by several years due to the civil conflict and purposeful delays of our "Judas."(Chapter 10)

A basic understanding of how H.E.L.P. operates is helpful. All trainings we provide are free. The cost of food and lodging are provided by host communities when our staff travels. Trainees receive free food, lodging, and one-way transportation for training held at our center. They pay for one way of the transportation, with some exceptions. Most other NGOs and government training pay attendees to show up for training.

We do not begin trainings and development in an area without an invitation. First, a pastor, leader, or group of believers recognizes a need in the community; the pastor or leader may even realize he needs to earn income to support himself and his family in order to have time to preach and teach. For example, after hearing about the trainings provided by our NGO, a pastor may approach one of our H.E.L.P. staff (national missionary) with a desire to improve income for the many malnourished families in his village through increased crop production. Or, the pastor may seek to improve life in a village through a non-formal education program for women, followed by training for village health workers and traditional birth assistants. Once invited, the H.E.L.P. staff reviews the needs, assesses community interest and support, and schedules the appropriate training class (lasting a few days to weeks). Unlike most organizations, we do not focus on a single area or region. We focus on areas without the gospel and without development, but we only work by request, guided by the Holy Spirit and prayer. Information about trainings and follow-up, as well as how lives are changed, is spread by word of mouth. From 1999 to 2003, most of the communities we served were within a day's travel of the headquarters, but each year the outreach has extended further and further. Trainings are often scheduled up to a year in advance and advertised simply by word of mouth; the geographic area we currently serve takes over two weeks to travel by vehicle (where accessible) and by foot.

Literacy

Literacy, (Fig 4.1-4.7) or non-formal education is the center of community development and also the center of Christian growth. In a culture with multiple gods and deeply rooted polytheism, tendency toward syncretism[45] is a real concern. In the Himalayas, people often

---

[45]   Syncretism refers to fusing the old religions and idolatry with Christianity.

initially come to faith in Christ through dreams, visions, demonic deliverance, or miraculous healings. Church leaders or pastors may be the only followers of Jesus in a village. In one instance, for example, an enthusiastic, illiterate pastor preached, "Jesus heals" but could not read the Scriptures to learn more. In other cases, we have observed that false teaching was introduced by immature church leaders (or deceivers) and those in their flock could not discern the truth because of their inability to read and study the Bible for themselves. If, as followers of Christ, our goal is to obey His command to make disciples of all nations, teaching those disciples the Bible is a necessity. To grow a national church independent of foreign missionaries or foreign money, new believers need tools for health and economic development. In the 21st century, the ability to read and write at a basic level is essential for spiritual and physical development of a national (indigenous) church.

H.E.L.P.'s literacy department is the forerunner of the other departments. We encourage all communities and churches that approach us for assistance to start by offering our literacy program—a non-formal education program including literacy, health, and business principles. These literacy students lead the way for further spiritual and physical development in their families and communities.

A potential teacher (facilitator) may submit an application requesting a class in his or her village or a neighboring village after ensuring a minimum of 20 students desire literacy training. If accepted as a H.E.L.P. literacy facilitator for the year, he or she is invited to come to a series of training sessions and is provided all materials and a small stipend. Like H.E.L.P. courses, the literacy program utilizes the trainer-of-trainers method. While using our materials, which address business, life skills, health, agriculture needs, and much more, the teacher facilitates discussion and begins introducing concepts to the community. As the students understand more and build relationships, they identify other needs in the community.

H.E.L.P. volunteer leaders and staff, from literacy facilitators to traditional birth assistants, must be committed followers of Christ. This ensures our vision and mission of loving Christ first and loving our neighbor as ourselves is foremost; it also ensures equal treatment, regardless of caste or income. However, the community at large benefits from the training either by receiving services (non-formal education, curative and preventive health services) or by receiving education and hands-on skills training in animal husbandry, agriculture, or income generation. Community groups such as farmer cooperatives include those from all religious beliefs, castes, and walks of life. In this way, the local church becomes the center of learning and leadership in the communities, raising the status of the few Christians to one of a reservoir of knowledge. While not in our original plan, this process has also helped to break down religious and cultural barriers, enabling communities to work together to survive—to cooperate in a mutually beneficial way—regardless of their beliefs.

Many of the churches and leaders we work with use these non-formal education classes as an outreach into areas untouched with the good news of Christ. A community that might be opposed to a church will usually not be opposed to a literacy class in their village. Once the class has been meeting successfully for a short time and the locals see the benefit, they realize that Christianity is not harmful; it is not a "foreign" religion and Christians actually help their community. Literacy classes also provide a way for more educated youths who have embraced faith in Christ to reach out to their community and develop leadership skills as they demonstrate the love of Christ to their neighbors. After the initial one-week training, during which they practice and interact with facilitators from other areas, they develop relationships with others from around the country as the H.E.L.P. full-time literacy staff observe them and teach them how to use the materials. The facilitators have fun learning how to teach as they fellowship with other believers, singing psalms and hymns, and encouraging one another. During the initial trainer-of-trainers class, representatives from each department meet new facilitators, explaining H.E.L.P. programs in health, environment, animal husbandry, agriculture, and economic development.

Following the initial teaching course, facilitators return to their homes and villages throughout the Himalayas and begin the non-formal education classes, which are held two hours a day, six days a week. They teach these beginning classes for three months, and then return for a refresher training course. During the first three months of classes, appointed leaders (including religious and local leaders) observe how students and teachers learn and ensure classes are properly conducted with good attendance of both teachers and students. H.E.L.P. group representatives (GRs) also check on the classes, as do staff from other departments who may be visiting the region. Multiple tiers of accountability support not only provide training in how to teach literacy and non-formal education concepts such as business and math, but also spiritual training and Bible study.

Our first literacy class in 1999 was attended by twenty-two students in a relatively developed town with private and government schools as well as easy road accessibility. Mrs. Bajracharya, who later became H.E.L.P.'s national director, invited acquaintances who had never had the opportunity to attend school. They varied in social status and in caste, though most were middle—to low-income status. Only a few were Christians; the rest were Hindus. In my first visit to their class, the ladies shared a bit about their lives—some were married at thirteen and bore a child at fourteen. Their lives were full of hardship and suffering. All shared the shame of being unable to perform basic math, read signs on the buses, read legal documents or newspapers, or help their children with simple schoolwork; they were embarrassed because they felt ignorant and unworthy. The young Christians expressed sadness that they were unable to read their Bible or hymn books in church.

Over the next six months, a phenomenal transformation occurred. Deep relationships developed among the women as they worked together in their struggle to learn. One young woman cried because each evening when she came home, her food was thrown away as punishment; her father-in-law forbade her learning to read. Most, however, received encouragement from their families. Their teacher became their confidant and guide to education in business, health, and agriculture. Though many previously knew each other, their shared goal to be able to read and write united them in a deeper friendship. One older lady, an ardent Hindu, had attended several classes taught by her husband and administered through a well-funded government program, but she had never succeeded in learning to read. Through the patient work of her Christian teacher, she learned to read and write. After her class, she scolded her husband: "My Christian teacher was better and more committed." She could see the love of Christ in her teacher, and though she did not follow Jesus, it changed her view of the believers, improved her life, and helped to break down caste and religious barriers. These women, previously shy and beaten down, were transformed during the class. At graduation one beautiful young woman confessed to me:

"I was blind, but now I can see."

Another composed a heartfelt poem expressing how her life was so much more full and alive now that she could read. During that first graduation, I begged God to allow us to give thousands more the opportunity to go from blindness to sight through literacy. He continues to do so.

Many of the ladies from this first class (as well as hundreds in later classes) went on to open shops, start small businesses, or help their young children with schoolwork. Previously they had been cheated in the market and were unable to relate with their children attending school, but now they held up their heads and led their children in learning. The process of transformation and the student/teacher relationship was much like what Jesus modeled with his disciples. Every student heard the gospel of Christ and received a first book as a gift—God's Word in their language. Several trusted Christ and became part of a local church; all learned the Christian faith was not one to be feared and shunned, but one in which love of neighbor is a central tenant. Within a few years, thousands of women throughout the Himalayas benefited through H.E.L.P. literacy programs, but these first classes impressed us with the importance of literacy and non-formal education as the backbone of community development.

Both initially, and even today, our classes differ in some ways from the standard approach of most development organizations. The typical courses run by the government programs and some NGOs are as short as three months, but in that time few students can read and write even their name. In the beginning, our basic classes were six months, with starting times adjusted to the growing season for crops. H.E.L.P. initially purchased materials in the local language used by many other NGOs and government classes. Since other classes were free (some even paid students to attend), our first classes were also completely free, with pencils, notebooks, and books supplied by H.E.L.P. As classes grew, however, leaders recognized the need for some buy-in on the part of students. We instituted an incentive system where each student pays a deposit, which is later returned at the completion of the course. If a student married or dropped out of the class, she forfeited the deposit, which was then managed by the women's group in the community. In addition, students purchased their own notebooks and paid a minimal fee (dependent on the income of the community) so that nothing was provided completely free. This initiated a feeling that H.E.L.P. classes are worth more, because they cost more; commitment of the teachers to the students has proved this true.

The literacy department developed rapidly over its first two years, particularly when God brought Mr. Shrestha, whose own vision expanded ours. (Chapter 6) He recognized the essential nature of literacy, particularly in elevating the status of women. After he taught his wife to read and write, she began an income-generating business for poor women in their church, as well as an outreach feeding street children. Neither of these endeavors received funding or direction from foreigners. From the inception, Mr. Shrestha realized the importance of proper training of our teachers. (Fig 4.1) He developed a hands-on practice teaching method where teachers came to the center, stayed for one week, worked, prayed, fellowshipped, and practiced using the materials together. This initial trial developed camaraderie among teachers and fostered confidence as they used the books and flip charts to "teach" their peers. Using the trainer-of-trainers methodology, he inspired them to not just teach at a high level of excellence, but to have the love of Christ for their students as they shared the Lord with them. At the end of the class, they held a solemn candle lighting ceremony passing the flame from their teachers to one another, with the light representing both the light of literacy illuminating the darkness of ignorance, and Jesus, the light of the world, illuminating spiritual darkness. (Fig 4.6)

During this time, God brought us another committed young man to develop the expanding literacy program, Mr. Ramtel. Though younger and less experienced, he had an equally devout commitment to bring his nation and unreached peoples to Christ through literacy and development, loving them in Christ's name. Within three years, the literacy classes expanded to districts well beyond our headquarters, and these two young men felt the need to write additional literacy texts that would incorporate stories of those who overcame illiteracy and poverty and came to know Christ. The first book written for advanced students, *My Soul,* contained stories and photos of people who had been blessed by H.E.L.P. ministries and who came to follow Jesus through literacy, agriculture, health, or animal husbandry training. These individuals freely shared—even prior to the freedom allowed by the present government—unafraid of the persecution they might endure. Two years later, while working closely with national literacy experts at the university, they produced a second literacy text, *Self-Reliant.* (Fig 4.4) Mr. Shrestha and Mr. Ramtel had traveled to various communities where we held literacy classes, asking communities about the content of the book and testing their level of literacy. This book focused not only on reading, but also on sanitation, health, environmental issues, family issues, business basics, and income generation. They felt that upon completing the class, students should have the materials to truly be self-reliant.

Initially, we chose literacy facilitators based on recommendations from churches and requests from communities. After four years, as demand for classes increased beyond our ability to supervise and fund them, we began holding interviews for the literacy facilitators at our

> **Prior to the trainer-of-trainers refresher seminar, each teacher is observed in his/her role and the literacy team receives feedback from community leaders on how classes are progressing.**

headquarters. As we spread to more distant areas, our staff traveled to interview applicants in four central locations around the country. Though our actual pay for teaching a class is minimal, significantly less than the government or other organizations, competition became intense as excited, young, educated Christians saw the opportunity to help their communities, improve their leadership skills, and share their faith.

The literacy program continues to evolve. Instead of focusing only on completion of a six-month course, we later divided sections of the class and adjusted books accordingly. We kept our six-month beginning course and added a second book to for a nine-month basic course, which we encouraged all students to complete. Though our goal was to have a full twelve-month course, those students who completed nine months of training generally did quite well. Classes were held six days a week for the first nine months, and twice a week for the remainder. After the first three months, teachers returned to H.E.L.P. headquarters for a second training session. Here they exchanged stories about teaching students, practiced teaching again, and learned how to use their second book, *Self-Reliant.*

After three months, most students were able to hold their pencil and read and write simple words; they were becoming more excited about their newfound knowledge and began learning more about health, environment, and business skills. Using *Self-Reliant* as a textbook, they completed a total of nine months in the basic literacy course. Exams were given at three, six, and nine months. Then, *My Soul* was taught two days a week. At each step, teachers returned for trainer-of-trainers program to discuss victories, problems, and issues with their classes. Depending on the community, altitude, and calendar for planting crops or national festivals, class schedules were adjusted to allow villagers (mainly farmers) to attend. Between the teachers' refresher trainings, Mr. Shrestha and Mr. Ramtel visited as many classes as possible to observe the teachers, helping them deal with students with learning issues and encouraging them spiritually.

When young girls or boys were in classes, their teachers helped them to enroll in a government school at completion, usually at a fourth grade level, allowing them to progress much more rapidly and to avoid the embarrassment of attending kindergarten at age twelve to fourteen. This was especially important in areas of Nepal deeply affected by the Maoist insurgency, as there were no schools open for these children to attend for many years.

As time progressed, the number of classes increased exponentially and their distance from our headquarters continued to increase; our full-time staff became more exhausted. Frequently they rode a bus for one or two days, and then walked several days to arrive at a village. To ensure accountability and save their health, the literacy team developed a method of utilizing colleagues in other departments to also check on the classes. As this system of group representatives (GRs) evolved, these leaders began surprise and planned visits to classes, giving feedback on quality of classes. Next, we began requiring a nearby pastor or church leader and/or a community leader to check on the class on a regular basis. If a teacher, or many students, were not attending the class, our staff were alerted and visited to find the problem. Any class that was not maintaining adequate attendance, or in which the facilitator became ill or could not teach, was closed. Thankfully, this rarely happened. This integrated system, coupled with our policy of giving nothing free, not only prevented our wasting money, but also involved multiple people from the community, providing the community buy-in essential for sustainable development. Maintaining high standards also brought pride to both the students and the teachers, and encouraged discipleship of both. (Fig 4.2, 4.5, 4.7, 10.5)

To assess the level and effectiveness of learning, we gave and continue to give exams. Literacy exams are not of the same stringency as classroom exams in a traditional school. Frequently, visitors might contribute a bit to the answers, and a schoolchild sitting with his mother can give a little assistance. Nevertheless, these exams assess how many students have a basic level of literacy at the end of three, six, nine, twelve months and even after. Top students and highly ranked teachers earn prizes, but all students completing the course receive a Bible (donated by Nepali Gideons) in the local language. Hindus, Buddhists, and especially Christians value this gift. In most areas, books in the local language are not readily available, and in addition to the small library we give to the classes for extra reading practice, the Bible and hymnbooks are the most valuable assets to assist in continued learning and reading, even beyond the completion of the class.

Since literacy classes provide a long-term opportunity for relationships, the other H.E.L.P. departments not only educate the literacy facilitators (teachers) during teacher training times at the headquarters, but also visit literacy classes to distribute information to communities about other trainings H.E.L.P. can provide. For example, if an area is suffering from diarrhea epidemics and has no toilets, a H.E.L.P. health worker visits the literacy class, asking if the community would like to invite the health team to teach on sanitation and toilet-building, as they learn about these issues in their literacy book. (Fig 4. 3) If another area has inadequate food supply through the year, the agriculture and animal husbandry teams visit to explain the trainings they provide, offer income generation classes, and assist the literacy class in organizing a farmer's cooperative. If a child's parents die and there are no close relatives to care for him or her, a literacy facilitator or GR informs the Jyoti Niwas (House of Light) children's home of the legitimate need. In the same way, if a child has a relative willing to care for him or her but that relative cannot afford to send the child to school, the literacy facilitator or GR requests information to refer to our coordinator for the Jyoti Jiwan (Light of Life) program to help with basic needs and encourage "foster" care.

True stories are the best way to capture the inestimable impact of the H.E.L.P. literacy department alone, both in terms of physical impact (empowering women to read, write, care for the children, run a business, prevent prostitution) and spiritual impact (hundreds of believers, new churches, and hostile neighbors no longer unfriendly). Each year we request teachers to submit, in the local language, some

> An integrated system is absolutely essential for literacy, as well as community development, including children's ministry and orphanage care. Without integration, the community will never become responsible for its own welfare, and compassion for the poorest will be deferred to foreigners who may or may not fund the social needs but will certainly never meet the spiritual needs.

stories of how their lives and the lives of their students have been changed through H.E.L.P. literacy classes. The following chapter includes a few of the hundreds we have received, translated into English. Interestingly, the stories they submit are often not only about how Christ changed their own attitudes and lives but also how He changed their students.

Health

Health (Fig 5.1-8, 9.1, 9.5, 10.4) is the second tenant of community development on which H.E.L.P. focused. I provided more direction; as a result, the health department was slower to develop strong indigenous leadership. Though I recognized the tremendous influence of all the other areas of life on health, as a family physician

I was still faced with the daily heartbreak of simple diseases which caused great suffering due to either lack of prevention or lack of early recognition and treatment. In no population did this become more evident than among pregnant women and children under five years of age, an area of public health and medicine referred to as maternal and child health. Rural areas of the Himalayan region have some of the highest maternal and infant mortality[46] in the world. Some of these deaths are due to a lack of operative facilities or simple treatments to prevent infection and stop bleeding. But as in most of the developing world, clean water, sanitation, and adequate housing are even more influential in affecting health outcomes than is curative medicine.

In the Himalayas, communities may be isolated and have virtually no access to curative care. A proliferation of private medical colleges, as well as many students traveling abroad to China and Russia to study medicine, means more medical doctors are available than in the past. Nursing schools and programs for allied health workers have also increased, but this has not improved conditions in most villages. Doctors, nurses, laboratory technicians, and hospitals are concentrated in the cities where a wealthier clientele live; even those with an altruistic spirit find it difficult to move to rural areas where simple amenities are unavailable and life is difficult. Poor government support of rural hospitals and clinics, few support staff, and a lack of medical supplies further discourages resource allocation to the poorest people. In Nepal, rural areas may have certified medical assistants (CMAs) and health assistants (HAs) who provide curative care and dispense medication. Auxiliary nurse midwives (ANM) and staff nurses provide most obstetric care not given by the mother-in-law of the patient.

---

[46] The maternal mortality ratio is the number of deaths within 41 days of delivery per 100,000 live births. The infant mortality is the number of deaths of children less than 1 year old per 1,000 live births.

Government health posts (clinics) are theoretically available to many, but often are unstaffed or lack supplies due to funding and geographic challenges. In larger towns and villages, medical shops dispense medication at a profit to the shop owner, who may have virtually no medical knowledge.

Sanitation is abysmal in cities and rural areas. With the exception of the more highly educated and wealthier class, few families or homes have a toilet of any sort. Pit latrines[47] (Fig 5.1) are the most practical and affordable option, but they can compound the spread of disease when placed too close to the water supply. Septic tanks and sewage treatment centers are extremely rare. In the mountains, water comes from a spring or lake, while in the lowlands, water frequently comes from wells. Both are often contaminated with bacteria, heavy metals, and human and animal feces. Piles of trash and refuse breed disease; a lack of coordinated trash disposal causes toxic materials and insecticides to accumulate in soil and water supplies. Most people still cook with open fires, a huge health hazard due to burns, fires, and smoke inhalation. At times, shortages of gas and kerosene necessitate a return to use of wood fires, even among the wealthy.

In H.E.L.P.'s health department, the leadership structure reflects the type of training. Health education, led by volunteers who live in the village, has been and is a demonstration of love, as Christians teach their neighbors how to prevent and cure common health problems. The main types of volunteers—who are unpaid but receive free training, refresher training, and follow-up visits—are traditional birth assistants (TBAs), maternal child health workers (MCHWs),

---

[47]   A hole dug in the ground with a bamboo or rock outhouse surrounding the hole, for use as a toilet. As running water is not available or reliable in most of the country, no water is required and when the hole is full, it is covered, and the stall can be moved.

and village health workers (VHWs, now more recently also called community health and sanitation workers). All of these function as community health evangelists, but rather than giving them this title, we teach that the evangelism is a natural outflow of their work in preventive (primarily) and curative health care. These volunteers are believers in Christ with a desire to serve their community. During their initial one-week training, our full-time staff have the opportunity to interact with them, disciple them, and teach them pertinent health material. Then, on regular follow-up either by the health team or other departments, as well as their periodically scheduled refresher trainings, we provide additional health training and spiritual discipleship. These men and women, in turn, serve as the hands and feet of Jesus in their local communities by teaching, healing, promoting sanitation, and sharing the gospel. Those of all religions participate in health education outreaches and benefit from the services of these volunteers.

Recognizing the health problems and the minimal access to health care, and following Christ's command to love God and love our neighbor, H.E.L.P. began to train village community health workers (VCHWs) for dual purposes—evangelism/discipleship and community health. The initial course for VCHWs lasts 5 to 7 days. We focus on teaching these young men and women, chosen by their church fellowship and community, about communicable diseases such as tuberculosis, leprosy, diarrhea, and pneumonia. The class curriculum includes early treatment of injuries, wounds, bites, and innumerable simple illnesses that can be treated cheaply and easily at the start, but may lead to life- or limb-threatening emergencies when left untreated. More emphasis, however, is on learning ways to maintain health as well as to understand the causes and prevention of diseases, rather than just the treatment.

The training includes hands-on teaching of how to build a simple toilet, prepare *sarbotam pitho* and build a *duwa rahit chulo*. Education on nutrition, sanitation, clean environment (trash disposal), and clean water (including simple, affordable means to decontaminate water[48]) are central. Initially, we equipped each VCHW with a basic medical kit, gleaning much of our information from programs in other parts of the country and neighboring countries. The kits included a de-worming medication, oral rehydration solution, materials for dressing wounds, a safe delivery kit

> **Innumerable people have been and are being treated and cured at an earlier level, preventing loss of life or limb, or disability, as well as being brought to faith in Christ through the simple, selfless love of these health volunteers trained by H.E.L.P. who are, in practice, community health evangelists.**

(sterile blade, piece of plastic, and string), paracetamol (acetaminophen), and a few other items. At the trainee's initial refresher course, if the H.E.L.P. health staff felt the VCHW was performing satisfactorily and there was no available health post, he or she was also given more advanced medications (such as an antibiotic, per protocols established by the department of health) to dispense. Only medications labeled in the local language and purchased in-country were used, both to ensure volunteers could read the labels, and to support local economy.

As in other departments, this training was first held at our training center. After three years, the communities we served were more remote and the health team traveled by foot and bus, carrying with them flip charts and illustrations, and using local foods to teach nutrition. By 2012, more than 80 percent of all trainings were in the local community. Over time, the use of kits and contents of those kits has

---

[48] This included solar methods (sodis), chlorine, etc. Unfortunately, boiling water is not always possible due to lack of wood.

also significantly changed. During the time of the Maoist insurgency, when our volunteers lived in areas with absolutely no health care, we provided more medications. Now, in areas with sufficient health posts[49] or clinics, we focus on working with them, rather than competing with existing facilities. We maintain good relationships with government and NGO facilities, making sure we do not duplicate services, but instead provide care to the poorest of the poor.

Early on, our health team recognized that preventive measures, health education, and sanitation must precede curative medicine, but in areas with no access to medical care, a VCHW must provide simple first aid or treatment of worms, diarrhea, and pneumonia. In areas with a nearby health facility, he or she often leads communities to work together to collect funds for a poor family who cannot afford more advanced care, or accompanies those who fear leaving their village to seek care where it is available. They identify communicable diseases such as leprosy and tuberculosis, and they utilize treatments provided at no cost through other organizations, so that we do not misallocate God's resources by duplicating services already available. Our VCHW volunteers have become so well respected that they are frequently chosen when there are government or community selections for a health worker in the village to oversee programs for communicable diseases. Immunizations are available through well-funded donor agencies, but locals often do not trust those interventions and will not immunize their children even during epidemics. VCHWs are from the village, have personal relationships and trust, and are often the link to bring these health measures to people who need them most but are unable or fearful to access them.

---

[49]   Government health posts were often not staffed during the years of Maoist insurgency. Even now the staffing and availability of medications varies greatly depending on the distance from the road and funding.

From the beginning, the CMA directing this program recognized that young leaders who received free VCHW training (or any of the H.E.L.P. health trainings) must model health prevention in *his or her own life* by building pit latrines next to and smokeless stoves in their own homes. The VCHW students themselves began friendly competitions to see whose village could build the most toilets, cleanest paths, and best sanitation programs, and they compared their success at refresher trainings. Free refresher trainings are held once or twice yearly to assess how much the students learned, how they applied their knowledge, and how the treated patients fared. Also, our full-time H.E.L.P. health staff, GRs, and staff from other branches follow up with the volunteers. The field follow-up and refresher trainings are key to maintaining the success and competency of our health volunteers.

Women most effectively reach other women and young children, but it is also critical to have male workers to influence men, who control most of the decision-making in the family and village. In addition, we found the men often have more time to provide basic health care and teaching on sanitation and environment. We make an effort to include many men as VCHWs, not only to encourage them to serve their communities, but also as their buy-in is essential for the implementation of health change in the family. Hundreds of our VCHWs, male and female, have continued to serve tirelessly as volunteers in their communities for the past twelve years. Others who were active for many years could not continue to attend refresher training, but still serve as resources for healing and education in their communities. All continue to teach others, including their own family, a better level of hygiene and basic health awareness. Each year, we add many more community health workers with a variety of titles as H.E.L.P. expands to new unreached regions of the Himalayas.

As we slowly developed the health program, I searched through materials produced by the government and other NGO sources for safe motherhood programs and investigated outreaches through the local hospital where I worked. As described in chapter 6, I was involved in teaching advanced obstetric and pediatric emergency care to national nurses, and to (and with) national doctors. Although the government and doctors were improving their training and treatment for women and children, millions were not able—geographically, culturally, or financially—to benefit. God brought Mrs. Magar, a lovely young woman already working with her husband in evangelism and discipleship in the church, to lead the way. She had a vision to reach her people with the good news of Jesus and a passion to educate women about health and nutrition during pregnancy, breastfeeding, and weaning. She, with the assistance of our two CMAs, Mr. Shah and Miss Tamang, developed a maternal-child health program, which I initially supervised and checked closely (over the first four years), similar to other programs in Nepal and in surrounding areas. The two major differences of the H.E.L.P. traditional birth assistant program (and later, maternal child health worker addition) was and is as follows: first, our volunteers have a deep commitment to Christ and an equally great desire to serve the women of all castes and social status in their surrounding village area, and, secondly, though unpaid, they are supported through our multi-tiered field follow-up, refresher, and accountability program.

For cultural reasons, we require TBAs to be married with at least one child. As few such women in rural areas are literate, we include illiterate women as well, encouraging them to pursue literacy in one of our classes. As our literacy program expanded, we found women are receptive to additional knowledge once they complete the literacy program, and we currently have more literate TBA candidates than when the program began in 2000.

As with every aspect of community development, we offer TBA training only to those communities who request help and to those who have poor access to obstetrical or infant care, always focusing on less-developed areas. Candidates apply for the volunteer position through a local fellowship of believers and must show a willingness to serve and learn. Unlike similar government, NGO, and INGO trainings, we do not pay volunteers to attend training or even to provide services, but they receive free training, follow-up, and field visits. They spend ten days learning basics of prenatal and infant care, pregnancy, delivery, and nutrition followed by refresher training once or twice a year. As with VCHWs, much of this is hands-on teaching: learning to make *sarbotam pitho*, practicing delivery and simple resuscitative measures with mannequins, and building a *duwa rahit chulo* to protect children from burns and women from smoke inhalation. Those in the neediest areas receive tools such as simple delivery kits with a sterile blade, clean string, and piece of plastic for delivery. Available for a few cents, these kits prevent neonatal tetanus by providing a clean blade and string; the plastic provides a barrier to decrease contamination from dirty areas where deliveries occur. Because of our focus on prevention, most of the training focuses on developing these women to be leaders in their villages, teaching them first and then demonstrating how they can teach others. They, in turn, form women's groups, hold weighing clinics to screen for malnutrition in children under five, and pass on their knowledge to more women, as well as their husbands and children.

Following initial TBA training, our H.E.L.P. nurse midwife and CMAs follow up in the villages of the TBAs, examine pregnant women with the trainees, and assist them in building relations with and working with (where available) both government workers and other NGOs involved in safe motherhood programs. Our TBAs, like the VCHWs, have been quickly recognized for their higher level of training, as well as compassion, and their willingness to deliver women of even the lowest caste. As Christians, they are not constrained by caste rules of cleanliness that would prevent a higher caste TBA from entering the home of a lower caste woman. The families and communities they serve often give gifts of food, money, or clothes, as they are able. The TBAs continue to receive expanded trainings, and those who do outstanding work become regional representatives, assisting newer TBAs in their regions. Some have been chosen by their communities to receive pay through government programs utilizing village women as maternal-child health workers.

As the needs of communities and regions change, our original TBA training expands and changes. In some regions, for example, there are few Christians, but Hindus and Buddhist women want health

> **Flexibility and responsiveness to the needs of an individual community are two key features that support the success of our maternal and child health programs.**

training. H.E.L.P. national staff and volunteers work with and through the local believers and provide one- and two-day health education classes to enable these women to better care for their families and themselves. These are widely attended and also bridge community relations between Christians and non-Christians; once more, the church is the source of knowledge and information. Thankfully, because of funding available from other agencies to decrease maternal mortality, some regions now provide a cash subsidy to women who present in labor for an "attended delivery" by a trained nurse midwife or CMA at the government health post. In these areas, we have replaced TBA training with more focus on MCHWs who serve in much the same role, except that they often accompany and support the pregnant woman so she will feel safe using more modern health methods that provide for supervised deliveries and lessen morbidity and mortality of mother and infant.

Building a base of volunteers and an intact accountability and referral system takes time. In the initial four years of our health team, I frequently accompanied Mr. Shah, Miss Tamang, and Mrs. Magar, examining patients with them. Later, as we began developing our volunteer TBA, VCHW, and MCHW workers, I watched them supervise their students. Medical clinics, which we generally tried to hold on a regular basis in a church or community facility, brought healing to individuals, but did not change the general health of the village. These "medical camps", however, did allow our organization and Christians in general to develop a reputation of caring for the sick, regardless of their ability to pay. They also broke down barriers in communities as Hindus and Buddhists realized they could enter a church meeting place or Christian home without being under a "curse." As I was actively involved in medical care at national hospitals, we also had a ready referral source for patients who needed more advanced care. Later, after I left Nepal, the NGO continued to develop relationships with facilities to care for patient's more advanced health needs.

In areas with no health care and no basic medications available, we adapted the health program to meet the needs. Once more, we depended on the national leadership and the local community, and we relied heavily on their input to make these decisions, a dependency that resulted in sustainability and growth. We also quickly recognized that we did not have the resources in staff, medicine, or facilities to provide curative care. Rather than investing in building more clinics or hospitals, which would likely not be sustainable for our partner NGO, we prayerfully decided to focus on prevention coupled with simple curative measures that could be taught to volunteers at a local level. Our relationships allowed us to refer patients to other NGO programs who, for example, could provide subsidized surgical procedures such as a hysterectomy for uterine prolapse. They valued our contacts at the village level since they could not always utilize their funds in the most effective way, as they were based in better-served urban areas.

During the early evolution of the health department, there were a few occasions when we accidentally offended community leaders and threatened the income of local medical shops. We quickly learned that for any outreach, we must inform and involve all levels of social and political leaders, and be sure not to hurt the existing businesses by providing free or subsidized medication in areas where it could be purchased. After the first three years, we slowly reduced the number of our outreach medical clinics and found that as we expanded community health, sanitation, income generation, and literacy education, the community's health needs dramatically decreased.

Personal field follow-up has proven to be one of the most effective means to encourage the hundreds of TBAs, MCHWs, and VCHWs who are essentially community health evangelists and receive no pay for taking time from their work and fields to examine, assist, and support their communities. H.E.L.P. health staff visit volunteers' homes, share stories, see difficult cases, and encourage them in their spiritual walk. GRs who live in the region also follow up when they are in the area, and in situations where more expertise is needed, they send word to H.E.L.P. health staff. This close network of accountability, teaching, and discipleship supports these volunteers continuing to serve Christ and their communities for years.

Many have testified, "I would have given up on my walk in Christ, and my service to the village, if H.E.L.P. staff and GRs had not visited me."

Both the health team and volunteers have given us hundreds of stories of how lives are changed. The next chapter includes a few stories to give a glimpse of the dramatic benefits.

Smokeless stove

One of the simplest, cheapest, and most effective interventions we have utilized in the area of health and environment has been the *duwa rahit chulo* or smokeless stove.

> The smokeless stove program is likely our most economical program with the greatest health and environmental gain.

(Fig 7.2, 10.6) This simple device can be made in many forms. The basic concept is that of a Franklin stove or fireplace, but using locally available materials. In most areas the stoves are made from mud bricks that can be molded, baked, and repaired in the village. Once the stove or chimney is designed for the appropriate altitude, releasing more or less heat, and fit for the size of the cooking pan, a pipe carries smoke from the stove through a conduit out the side of the house. This simple device not only dramatically decreases accidents from fire and burns to babies and children, but also decreases smoke inhalation, which is known to cause chronic lung disease in women and children. Because the mud molds to the pan and the vent from the stove cooks more efficiently, use of the stove decreases time spent collecting firewood, giving women more time to learn to read and care for their families. Greater efficiency also decreases deforestation by reducing the number of small trees harvested for wood. In addition, using ash, and compost materials with a mold, a briquette can be made which replaces wood and provides fuel for up to a day of cooking. These briquettes not only conserve word, but provide farmers income, selling them at the market (Fig 6.5). Virtually every department includes hands-on training of how to build these stoves during or after their classes, and most communities soon convert from open fires to these improved cooking methods.

Agriculture

When we began the animal husbandry and agriculture programs, we focused on believers (as per our Biblical mandate), but we soon found that limiting training to Christians caused community division. The local community and those embracing all religions benefit from the programs led by local believers. All community members are welcome to attend teaching about ginger cultivation, improved rice planting, pesticide-free farming, goat raising, or water buffalo health. They are informed, however, that it is a Christian-based training, and that there will be Bible study and prayer. As a result, the community better understands the Christian faith, is not pressured into any decision, and respects the church and believers who share information and skills to improve their lives. Farmer cooperatives and groups are generally centered around a local church, if there is one, but non-Christians are welcomed. The result has been a tremendous growth in followers of Christ and reduced persecution against new believers as neighbors see the physical benefits they reap. (Fig 6.1-6.6)

Follow-up training is essential. In fact, evaluations from trainees in health, agriculture, and animal husbandry repeatedly state: "You are different from other groups. You do not just have a class or teach; you follow up in the field. You care." (Fig 9.4, 9.2)

In agriculture, our first trainings focused on pesticide-free farming and increased production for consumption or profit. Our agriculturalist, Mr. Prajapati, saw the need early on to convince young people that farming *can* be profitable. He also saw the devastation in the Himalayan region from landsides due to deforestation and heavy contamination of water supplies by pesticides, recognizing that these were more than environmental issues; they also were damaging the productivity of the land and enslaving millions to poverty. In order to prevent the "brain drain" of young, energetic students who surpassed their parents in learning to read and write, graduating from class ten, or even attending college, he felt there must be a way to make the land produce crops—cash crops. Poor food production from tiny parcels of worn-out land affected the entire family's health. As I had seen with my patients, a single season without rain meant many people could not survive. A bad harvest would be followed by a measles epidemic that killed many children and increased tuberculosis cases, due to the low immunity caused by malnutrition. Within the first year of the agriculture programs, we witnessed the positive impact that improved agriculture practices had on the health of communities that requested training.

Improving composting methods is the basis of our sustainable agriculture program. Effective microorganism (EM) is a well-studied method first introduced in Asia. (Fig 9.6) It seemed a possible simple option for improving composting, benefiting animal health, reducing waste, and promoting pesticide-free vegetable production. H.E.L.P. sent both Mr. Prajapati and Mrs. Bajracharya to Thailand to receive training, and within two years, our NGO became the forerunners in EM utilization in Nepal. The agriculture team began to introduce this technique, which uses bacteria to speed the decomposition of compost and improve smells, decrease refuse, and enrich soil, through the local farmer groups.

Each year we have added more and more training classes depending on the needs of the community. Some years we have given more classes in floriculture and fruit tree planting, other years we added more classes on increased vegetable production or composting. In more crowded urban communities, we focused on kitchen gardens—small gardens which could be maintained with tiny plots of land, and yet provide needed nutrients to the family, or even cash crops. Growing mushrooms provides cheap protein and good income for hundreds of destitute families who had minimal land, but have an area suitable for fungus growth.

As the scope of the agriculture program grew, Mr. Prajapati developed the group representative (GR) program. Though later we began to use GRs in every department, they were initially trained through the agriculture program. GRs that lived close to the target communities could follow up with trainees in remote areas more quickly and reliably, making sure those attending the training really could implement the techniques they had learned.

Initially and even today, Mr. Prajapati follows up personally. Participants in trainings who demonstrate exemplary leadership and aptitude are chosen as GRs, like extension agents for H.E.L.P. staff. They receive additional free training and on-the-job assistance in multiple disciplines. GRs then follow up on the participants' understanding of what they learned and on their spiritual growth. As with other departments, their role in animal husbandry and agriculture training has become increasingly important because H.E.L.P. programs have spread to areas many days' travel from our headquarters. Each department also cross-covers for one another to follow up on practical outcomes of the knowledge gained. For example, after a literacy class has started in an area, if a health worker is in the area, he or she will stop in to see how the literacy class is progressing, and give feedback to the literacy trainers. After a training class on floriculture, the animal husbandry staff or a GR will check to see how the students are succeeding in their plant nursery. With each step, there is not only a follow-up of the quality and success of the program, but also on the spiritual growth of the students and leaders.

Hand-in-hand in the development of the GR program was formation of local farmer groups or cooperatives. Many communities, fractured by caste and religion, had no sense of cooperation. As H.E.L.P. demonstrated the need to share ideas, these farmers recognized their need to share seeds, simple equipment, and even money. We began training classes to form farmer groups, including skills such as choosing officers, accountability with money, and dealing with conflict. Our GRs followed up after formation to help solve problems and help the farmers work together. Farmer groups also served as host for farmer field schools.

Because crops grow over a period of time and farmers quickly get discouraged with new techniques that could threaten their production on small parcels of land, Mr. Prajapati began farmer field schools. A farmer field school is a hands-on community school in a farmer's field that lasts through the growing season. A willing farmer offers a plot (usually after visiting our experimental plots in the training center or witnessing success in another area) in which to grow a crop using EM and other new, sustainable techniques. Our H.E.L.P. agriculturalist stays for a longer time and makes frequent visits, working through the season with the community until the harvest. Farmer groups formed one year can choose another crop the following year, so they function as a sort of continuing education in the field for local farmers. These farmer cooperatives and field schools are so successful that the country's ministry of agriculture has recognized our NGO.

One of the main reasons the farmer cooperatives and field schools have been so effective is because H.E.L.P. works through the churches. There is a level of accountability and absolute right and wrong, and an acceptance of all castes. Those of all religions are welcome into the training and group. In addition, many of the Hindus and Buddhists of the community later follow Christ, through the sharing and witness of their neighbors, and are better able to understand each other and work in a spirit of community.

Not all of our experiments have been as successful as the farmer cooperatives and field schools, however. In fact, one impetus to form the farmer groups was the need (as we perceived) to provide loans for economic improvement

> **The Farmer's fair provides an opportunity to show-off the best crops and animals, and the Folk Festival provides fun competition as farmers compose songs and dances teaching new agricultural principles. (Fig 9.3)**

with group management. Our initial attempts to provide low-interest loans to farmer groups produced less than ideal results. Though the amounts of money were small, the temptation for an individual to use his loan for a more pressing need (the marriage of a relative, for example) was too great. This left the borrower unable to repay and resulted in more fractured relationships and even caused spiritual damage due to unwillingness to fellowship with others out of guilt. After several years of teaching communities how to appoint officers, manage a ledger (account), and share responsibility, the cooperatives themselves began individually donating within their group, and H.E.L.P. assisted them by training them to manage their own treasury. This has been much more successful, with nearly 100 percent payback since there is peer pressure within the farmer groups to not default on a loan from a neighbor, and the group knows how much is safe to loan to a given individual! We had a similar experience when we tried a program to gift animals, a common practice by many organizations.

Interestingly, many practices touted by highly funded aid organizations, which have intellectual and visual appeal (such as giving an animal), have not been successful in our experience.

Along with the animal husbandry team, the agriculture team began writing and printing pamphlets and booklets almost immediately. These booklets have proved invaluable as sources of information, and indirectly they have elevated the level of the farmers, as those with more education have material to read. In addition, the booklets provide a valuable resource to the country as a whole. Before we began publishing these booklets, almost no material was available in the local language at a simple reading level. Mr. Prajapati, encouraged by the spiritual and physical success in the spread of agriculture training, suggested we try publishing a simple magazine on a quarterly basis. Soon, *Vineyard* was being read from the base of Mount Everest to the border of India. This popular quarterly farmer's magazine contains recipes, new composting techniques, and even personal testimonies of how farmers found the true God.

As the agriculture program expanded to multiple trainings in distant locations, the team realized the need to provide a showcase for the farmer groups in the form of a *mela* (farmer's fair). At the fair, churches and farmer groups compete for titles like the biggest pumpkin, healthiest goat, best handicrafts made from local materials, and much more. An exciting time for farmers all over the country to meet, they also share ideas, fellowship, and learn from one another.

Another purely Nepali tradition (suggested by our Nepali agricultural team) is our farmer folk festival. (Fig 9.3) This festival, which has been held annually for seven years, began with a handful of farmer groups and today includes hundreds. Throughout the year, groups compose songs praising God and sharing how they have come from poverty to sustenance, as well as explaining the farming methods they changed to do so. The songs are in a traditional Nepali style, sung using the *madal* (Nepali drum), and accompanied by traditional dancing and lots of joy. Held at the training center, this two- or three-day festival is a time of celebration. Locally known Christian musicians judge the compositions and performances, awarding prizes to the winning groups. In addition to providing fun and fellowship, these songs teach important principles, both spiritual and agricultural. Talent varies from ear-piercing singing that brings laughter, to true musical and dancing ability. All are welcome in a joyous celebration. Those from all religions and farmer groups participate, often traveling days to join the festivities.

The overall impact of the agriculture program is difficult to quantify, especially in a subsistence economy. Moving literally thousands of families from starvation to self-sustenance has been phenomenal, and is testimony enough to the far-reaching influence of our investments. Giving the gospel as we teach new and sustainable agriculture practices is not just a part of the process. From the very first training classes, we received requests for even more Bible study and prayer. Field follow-up for farmers provides the opportunity for GRs and H.E.L.P. staff to give the farmers spiritual and physical food for growth. Included in the next chapter are a few of hundreds of translated accounts from GRs and H.E.L.P. agriculture and animal husbandry staff, as well as from farmers and their families whose lives have been transformed by the gospel and better, sustainable farming techniques.

Animal Husbandry

Though the animal husbandry department (Fig 7.1-6) began shortly before the agriculture department, the two are closely integrated. Both departments have their own training classes, but they provide follow-up for each other. Generally, one or the other will give initial training classes in a community, depending on which needs are greater. Because of the small initial investment and potential income from selling goats, as well as the demand for goat raising, this was our focus for the first two years. After Mr. Acharya and Mr. Raju completed their training and certification as veterinarian technicians, they began training in additional areas most likely to provide income generation—poultry and swine. Soon after, we added classes on water buffalo health, because the death of such an expensive animal can result in financial ruin for a family. Each year we adapt training to meet the needs of the communities we serve. Preventive care training includes topics such as building proper sheds (off the ground to prevent hoof rot), using manure, feeding proper foods to animals, breeding, castrating, immunizing, and making mineral blocks. With only one veterinary school in a country with most families of any means owning livestock, we recognized it was essential for the average person to know basic animal care. In addition, we focus on the interaction between humans and animals, teaching prevention of common zoonosis[50] and challenging the traditional practice of housing animals on the lower floor of the house.

As more communities saw the income potential and food benefits from healthier animals, demands for our services far surpassed our ability to provide training. As with the agriculture department, we began utilizing GRs for follow-up, but we needed more. As some young men and women showed great aptitude, H.E.L.P. provided scholarships for them to become veterinary technicians as well, and though we did not give them any salary, they were able to have a good income through their veterinary outreach, as well as to provide follow-up for us in areas near their homes, supervising and assisting

---

[50]   A disease that can be spread from animals to humans.

in our trainings. As there are also no veterinary medications available outside of large cities, we provided at-cost or subsidized medications and vaccines through the technicians and GRs. Currently we focus more on helping communities to embrace preventive techniques and methods than on treating illness in the animals.[51]

Hundreds of families have written testimonials and stories about how their lives were changed by food and income generated from their animals, as well as by the transformational gospel they received. Many bi-vocational pastors are able to better support themselves by raising livestock, freeing up time to give congregations spiritual food. These hundreds of spiritual leaders do not need support of a foreign church or organization and are able to minister effectively in their own culture. This multi-tiered accountability and follow-up process is critical for both the physical and spiritual success of each department.

Environment and Sanitation

Critical to the development of any community program, especially one that values health, is a focus on maintaining the environment and sanitation. Though we have never created a separate department for this purpose, each department has always been involved in this focus. For example, literacy student workbooks contain a section on the importance of proper deposition of trash and sewage, maintenance of clean water supplies, instruction on toilet construction, pictures of a "clean" village, and call to action for removing human or animal waste from living areas. During or after literacy classes begin in an area, we witness clean up campaigns driven by the students, in their desire to put their new knowledge into practice. Written, and more

---

[51]   Recently we have been providing less medication as our staff find that when we do so, preventive methods are compromised. Instead, they utilize the budget more effectively by prevention of animal disease.

importantly, hands-on instructions for building toilets is a part of sanitation emphasis, even prior to formal health teaching. The use of EM in the agriculture and animal husbandry programs to rapidly decompose rotting vegetation or waste, not only enriches the worn-out soil, but also removes smell and disease generated by the waste. Using animal feces for generation of energy through innovative means[52] preserves the good while eliminating the bad aspects of animal waste. Teaching crop rotation, soil testing, and natural fertilizers[53] all enrich the environment for future generations. The smokeless stove program decreases destruction of forests by conserving wood, as well as providing knowledge on alternatives for fuel such as "charcoal briquettes." These unique briquettes are fashioned with a mold, and mixed from ash, egg shell, and other disposed of items, with the recipe taught to an industrious but poor farmer in each area we work. The briquette program provides a family with a regular income, and the market, with a cheap, sustainable alternative to wood.

Additional Income Generation

Because of the instability of the governmental structure, particularly during our early years, we focused on income generating efforts which did not require a middle-man, reliable transportation, or an international market. This limited our choices to those which could provide both for the needs of the household, and could be purchased

---

[52]   "Goober gas" is a method usable in lower altitudes through which methane in animal manure is converted to energy.

[53]   Harvesting animal urine for urea-based fertilizer, collecting animal manure and plant debris for enriching soil, and recycling ash in briquettes are but a few of hundreds of sustainable interventions our staff teach, which have the side-benefit of effectively using waste and keeping the environment more healthy.

by the nearby neighbors. In a primarily subsistence-based agricultural area, this led our focus to the agriculture and animal husbandry departments. Within those areas many of our basic training programs provided knowledge and skills so the farmers could grow sufficient vegetables, mushrooms, fruit trees, herbs, goats, chickens, swine, etc. to feed their families and sell the excess. In some areas, where communities had a demand and a need, we began classes in candle making and sewing, both of which have been successful in improving availability of commodities to local communities and increasing the income of those who make them.

Biblical Principles

1. *Just as we cannot separate the work of the branch from the true vine, we can separate the work of a Christ-based development program from Christ.* (John 15:1-17).

2. *Each branch of community development is just as important as the other, just as each member of the body of Christ is important to the total functioning of the body.* (I Corinthians 12:12-26)
   "The body is a unit, though it is made up of many parts; and though all its parts are many, they for one body. So it is with Christ." I Corinthians 12:12

3. *In studying the pattern of missions taught by the Apostle Paul in his missionary journeys, he taught, discipled, and followed up.* The same principles are implemented in the multiple accountability system that H.E.L.P. uses in each department, and between departments. (book of Acts)

Chapter 8

Changed Lives: True Stories

Because certain areas of the country are still sensitive to Christian work, we have changed the names of some individuals and avoided specific descriptions of their locale. Most of these people we have met personally. We have visited these villages, and have documentation verifying the truth of not only these stories (translated from Nepali) but also hundreds more.

Literacy

Teacher (facilitator) transformation stories

Binu

"My name is Binu. Because of God's blessing and grace, I received new life from Jesus. One day, I got a chance to teach illiterate mothers, sisters, and brothers in my church and town through H.E.L.P. When we teach, we can also share the gospel and love of our Lord Jesus. Because of God's light, I had an opportunity to teach and share the gospel to other people. I am very thankful to God. Before teaching a literacy class, I did not know all the people from my church or the people from the community. I did not even know their language, traditions and culture. I am a Magar (caste) and these participants were Chaudharis (caste), with a very different language and culture. Besides this, the class was a long walk and it was hard work to teach them. Even with the difficulties I still wanted to go there and share the gospel to those people because God called me for that . . . . I tried my best, thinking about God's love for me and in the same way I started to love them. Slowly, they opened up to me. I was more encouraged and also started to learn their language and their culture. We started our class hours and lessons with prayer but Satan brought the problems regularly. By God's grace, four people accepted Jesus Christ as their Savior . . . I was so happy because my main objective of going to that place and teaching was to share the gospel. Suddenly one day, I got very sick. I went to a doctor and the doctor diagnosed me with paralysis. I could move only one hand. I could not ride my bicycle now and had to walk an hour on the road. During that time, I cried so much because of pain and swelling of my leg. I had surgery on my leg. But still, I prayed so much and walked every day to the village. The road was mostly deserted and I used to walk alone; I had an opportunity to talk with God and to be closer to Him. Because of the participant's encouragement and love, I was more encouraged and confidence grew in me. Then I realized that when doing God's work, Satan will bring lots of problems, because he doesn't like it. I received strength and blessing from God and encouragement from the participants. Slowly, my health problems improved. During my class period, I learned many things and also taught them those things. I received respect and love from people around the village as well as the participants. *God is great! There is nothing impossible for Him. If it is God's will and we accept His will, we can be successful no matter what types of problems arise. We should not work with our own power, but need to work in God's power.* God is always with us. I took a step to teach the people and I was able to succeed so I will never forget this moment in my life. I also realized that we must educate people and show them the light!"

Samuel

"I am Samuel. First of all, I would like to give thanks to our living God, because according to His plan and will, I have succeeded. Our literacy class was started in a village where only a few Christians resided. The community people used to hate the Christians and caused them many problems. The believers were not invited to any social gatherings, weddings, or parties. When we thought about offering a literacy class from H.E.L.P., people opposed it. They told us that the literacy class was just a way to make everybody Christians and they didn't like it. They even threatened the willing participants should they go and join. We prayed continuously for this class but only had sixteen participants willing, and H.E.L.P. required twenty. Still we prayed. When the day came for the facilitator (teacher) interview, I was selected. I came for the training at H.E.L.P. headquarters and returned back to my village. Then, we invited some concerned educated people and authorities of the village for an opening ceremony of the class. They hesitated to come, but did. In the opening ceremony we showed them the literacy book. They were surprised since they thought we were going to teach from the Bible. They were feeling wrong and ashamed. In the opening ceremony they gave a speech saying that everyone must be literate and gain knowledge. On the first day there were only ten participants but the next day thirty-five came to class to take the book. God listened to our prayers and the number of participants increased beyond our thinking . . . we had to turn some students away as we did not have enough books . . . . At that time there were only nine believers. To conduct a home fellowship, we had to ride 17 km on a bicycle at night. Now that we had the H.E.L.P. literacy class, everything has changed. We have forty-five new members who have accepted Jesus Christ, and twenty-seven have already been baptized. Two of them were in the literacy class. *These days, people of the village look and treat us positively. The hate and disrespect has finally changed to love and respect. Christians are also invited to social gatherings and I am also able to do more of His service without any problems and fears. This is the success I have received from the literacy class."*

Madav

"My name is Madav. Before I started literacy class, many people from this area were unable to read and write. One day my pastor asked me if I could teach a literacy class . . . I started to talk with the people of my village. They were enthusiastic about the idea . . . Adults were enthusiastic to learn. I shared the gospel with them. Then, they came to know who Jesus is and when we believe in Him we will have eternal life. Before, in the village, people used to see Christians differently. But now they started to say that Christians are honest, their love is different from others and they are social workers. They learned all of this from the literacy class. Now the female participants are able to read the Bible, other books, and write letters. Not only that, they are able to speak in public and their self-confidence has increased. The participants tell me gratefully that they are fortunate to participate in this literacy class. *They also look forward to work for the betterment of the society. They want to uproot the caste division which still prevails in the community. Through the literacy class it has become easy to share the gospel and spread the Good News.* While I was teaching I not only taught from the book, but I shared the gospel. Two students accepted Jesus. I was able to go door to door and share, because of the literacy class. The students have formed an agriculture group and started a savings program. Now my students are literate and happy; many will now send their children to school and live a healthier life."

J. Tamang

"First, I would like to give thanks to our living God who loves us so much. Because of his plan, he took me to serve in a remote area. While I was doing evangelistic work, I had to face many difficulties. In one village I knew I must spread the gospel, but it was not easy. I met a H.E.L.P. group representative and learned about the work. I was selected in the interview to be a literacy facilitator, but in the village, people were against the class thinking I would teach and change the people to Christianity. They made plans to stop the class. But God is great. By his grace, we prayed and started the class. Now one family accepted Jesus and six people have been baptized. We have started fellowships in a few places as well. We are so thankful from our church that H.E.L.P. has given us this literacy class."

Shova

"I am from a simple farming family and followed Jesus from 2001 . . . In 2003 my father left our family. My life became more challenging than before. I had to take responsibility of my mother and my two younger sisters . . . Then, my pastor gave me the opportunity to become a literacy facilitator for H.E.L.P. I began a literacy class . . . villagers changed their negative view about Christians . . . They realized that literacy class opened their inner eyes. Now I have become a mother of those mothers and have to hear and pray for their problems . . . . I formed a farmer group through the literacy participants. We established a saving fund and collected money each month. We provided loan to needy members to run a shop and purchase male goats. H.E.L.P. provided us goat, poultry, vegetable, and health training. Then the literacy members started keeping goats, poultry, and swine. Some opened small shops, some are busy with vegetable farming, and others learn other technology from us . . . . Some began counseling on health issues and organized health outreaches and awareness programs. Before our literacy class there were only a few believers, now there are 80-100 in regular fellowship mainly due to our literacy class."

Student (participant) transformation stories

Subhadra

"My name is Subhadra and I am forty-five years old. My brother studied a little but we sisters didn't get a chance to study because society thought it useless to send girls to school. I did house work, goat keeping, grass cutting and other kinds of work from my childhood. I married at age 16 and now have 2 sons and 1 daughter. One time I became sick, and went to the hospital . . . I did an operation . . . but I was soon suffering from another sickness. Satan attacked me. Many witch doctors tried to cure me, but without success. Then, one of my relatives started a literacy class in my village. I wanted to go to the class, so I registered my name and went there to study. I felt happiness when I came back from the class . . . before I couldn't sleep well and always an unknown pain hit me. I think I got better due to the prayer before the class. I also started to search about God. I received Jesus Christ as my Lord and Savior during the literacy class and I started to go to church regularly. All the church members prayed for me. I also started to pray, and in this way, I am totally healed. Now I can read and write, I can read the Bible and other books. I can do mathematics problems. *Literacy class totally changed my life. I am able to know the Lord Jesus and I get the light of knowledge, as well.*"

K. Tamang

"My name is K. Tamang. I always wanted to read and write, but it was very difficult to go to school in my childhood. We had to walk more than three hours to reach the school; my parents didn't allow me to go. We had to work very hard in the village . . . caring for sheep and goats. Now, I had a chance to not only get education, but also to know about agriculture, livestock, health, and other important skills. Our teacher taught us through games, role play, and song. Now many Christian women can read their own Bible and sing hymns. Three families received Christ during the literacy class. *Villagers are also starting to think positively about Christians and their awareness level is increasing.* Now I am able to purchase and sell goods and keep records. I can write letters to my relatives in the city. Thanks to God."

Mina

"My name is Mina, and I was born in Rolpa district (a remote area of western Nepal). My father has two wives and my mothers had ten sons and five daughters. I am the first daughter of my father's first wife. In our society girls are never sent to school. They say that sending daughters to school is like cutting feet with your own axe. That is why I had to do all the household work, collect wood from the forest and cut grass for the animals. When I saw my brothers going to school, I also wanted to go to school. I cursed myself for being born as a daughter . . . . Then I got married, and my husband was attending school . . . We had two children and I vowed to myself to make my children literate. Sometimes I felt very bad when they asked me some questions during their homework time. It was good news when a sister in a nearby church was going to start an adult literacy class for two hours every day in the afternoon. I went and enrolled my name; I was very happy. At home, my husband also helped me during my studies. Now, I can write a simple letter, add and subtract . . . *this literacy class encouraged me that I can do something in the future.*"

G. Magar

"My name is G. Magar. I live in Udaypur. There were seven in our family; we were very poor so my parents could not send me to school . . . . One of our church brothers started an adult literacy class. I had a desire to study and be literate, so I went and started to study in that class. It was a one year literacy course, but I learned many things within nine months. I wanted to learn more and more now. I thought I must go to join in the school. Then one day I went to the school. After knowing my capacity the teachers suggested I enroll in class five. So, nowadays, I am going to school! *My life would have been spoiled if H.E.L.P. had not given a literacy class in our village.*"

Radhika

"My name is Radhika. I was born in Sindhupalchowk district . . . an only daughter of seven members. My parents said I must learn housework. I got married but my father-in-law died because of his beliefs in not going to the hospital. After marriage, I had three children and had a very hard time taking care of my family due to our poor condition and village. Then, I heard there was going to be an adult literacy class. After joining and studying . . . I can read and write. Because a Christian started the class, I had an opportunity to hear about Jesus. I started to learn how to pray and came to know about Jesus's mission in this world. *Then, I came to know that Jesus is my Savior . . .* and accepted Him."

P. Kumari

"My name is P. Kumari and I was born in Kapilvastu district. When I was small my parents used to stay in others' house as their servant. When I was a little grown up, my parents kept me as a servant in another house because my parents were so poor. I had a huge desire to be literate. When I saw other children going to school, I felt very sad. One day the government gave a literacy class in our village, but my parents did not let me go . . . I felt shame. One day I got married . . . and in my husband's village a literacy class started. My husband gave me permission to go and join in the class. I put all my effort to learn the alphabet, words, and then sentences. This literacy class (through H.E.L.P.) was much different than that by the government. In this class the teacher taught nicely. In a few months I could read and write. Now I can write a letter and do simple mathematics. *Now I am a member of women's development organizations and have taken livestock and sewing training.*"

Rupa

"My name is Rupa M. I was born into a poor family with eight children. As the youngest daughter in our family, everyone loved me, but we were poor and could not go to school. I felt like going to school when I saw my friends going. At fifteen, I got married . . . I did not know about marriage . . . I was playing outside with my friends, then my father called me inside and did some simple marriage ceremony and sent me with my husband. At my husband's home there were two daughters, one son, my mother and father in law. No one cared for me because I did not give them much dowry; I got scolding and beating from them all the time and did not get enough food to eat. At one time I was going to commit suicide, but because of my one son, could not do that. My life was in darkness. Sometimes when I saw my husband studying something, I also wanted to read. I asked him to teach me, but he never cared. I had an inner desire to read and write. One day I heard someone was going to teach literacy in our village. When I heard this I was very happy. That time I was staying in my parent's house. From there only I enrolled my name and started going to that class. I continuously went to class and studied . . . because I went to study every day my husband and family members started to quarrel with me. One day my teacher came to my house to visit me. My husband's sister scolded my teacher, but she stayed calm and told them to send me every day in the class. I continued to go and learn. I decided to attend even if my family members beat and scold me. Now I am able to read and write and can do simple math. I am twenty-two years old and have one daughter and one son. *Now I have a hope of doing something in the future and becoming self-reliant.* I would like to request parents not to marry their daughters at an early age . . . if she is illiterate then send them to literacy class. Thank you so much to H.E.L.P. and to my teacher Pampha."

Health

Stories from Village Community Health Workers (VCHW)

Santosh

"I am Santosh and I did not know anything about medicine and sickness before. I now teach my villagers and specially teach them to make *sarbotam pitho* (high protein flour for malnutrition). Many people asked how much money I receive for helping them get knowledge and treat diseases. *I tell them I did not receive a single penny . . . I am collecting money in paradise. This is the love of Christ!*"

Purna

"I am Purna. I was born in Okhaldhunga district, in a far, undeveloped village. I searched for God from age twelve and continuously read the Hindu books . . . Then, I heard about Jesus, but could not believe . . . I used to hate the people who came to tell the gospel . . . one day I heard the good news, believed, and . . . returned to my village . . . people were against me. I got an opportunity to take village community health worker (VCHW) training. After the training, I gave health awareness to our villagers. From our village the health post is one hour walk, *so people come to me for dressing wounds, fever, diarrhea . . . day by day many are coming.* Then I asked H.E.L.P. to come and teach more people in our village."

Bhojraj

"My name is Bhojraj. I have three daughters, three sons, one daughter-in-law and my wife in my family. We are farmers and I am an elder in my church in a small village. I got an opportunity to attend the village community health worker training. I did not have a toilet (outhouse) in my home, so after I finished training and went back home, first I built a toilet by my house. I did not have knowledge about health and hygiene, uses of toilet, so my house and surrounding area used to be very dirty. This training opened my eyes and I was feeling shame . . . *to give the education to others first I should change myself.* Then I started teaching my neighbors and all village people. In my village there were no toilets, so first I talked with the people about use of toilets and built fifteen simple toilets myself. In my village the children are so dirty . . . I started collecting the children giving the education . . . I also talked with people about diseases like diarrhea, pneumonia, and typhoid. *Because of this health program, many people received Jesus Christ.* Thank you, Lord, for giving me such an opportunity to serve the people and the Lord."

A. Magar

"My name is A. Magar. I live in Udaypur district. I am very interested to hear about health from my childhood. I want to keep my village clean, but all my desires are not fulfilled due to lack of knowledge. One day our pastor associated with the H.E.L.P. farmer group told us that we could receive VCHW training. I was trained in 2007. Then, in 2008 I received training as a traditional birth assistant. I want to thank our Lord for this opportunity. These trainings helped me to serve my villagers. I am providing advice to pregnant women, help them to visit the health post and take vaccines . . . tell them to eat green vegetables, fruits, lentils, fish and a balanced diet . . . I teach them about spacing their children and family planning. I treat people with diarrhea, headache, fever, and wounds. I provide health teachings on burns, cuts, and wounds . . . I teach how to clean the drinking water and why we should wash our hands before eating and after coming from the toilet. *Now villagers love and respect me. May the Lord bless the organization to reach other remote places like my village."*

A. Silwal

"My name is A. Silwal. Health training has become a benefit for me and my family. My village is the victim of a witch doctor as it is in a remote area. So, I started to create awareness on health and sanitation after my training. *Due to the idea that diarrhea is caused from the excess of water in the body, people do not provide water when their child is suffering from diarrhea.* I tried to counsel them and make them use *jivan jal*[54] and teach them how to make it, but they went to the witch doctor. One day a man cut his leg and came to my house and asked me for help. I washed his wound and bandaged it. After three days the wound was completely healed. From that day everyone was aware of the importance of the medicine. Then villagers often come to me when suffering. I give them treatment and advice for general diseases and if it is serious I take them to a clinic. I want to share an incident in my family. My father was a drunkard . . . he suffered from fever, cough, and blood in his cough. Because of my training, I thought it might be tuberculosis, and sent him to get a medical checkup. It was TB, and now he is almost cured . . . I am very thankful to God and to you."

Sita

"My name is Sita. After I took my VCHW and TBA training from H.E.L.P., I'm working in four different VDCs.[55] I teach health awareness, nutrition, safe drinking water, about toilets, and about mother and child health . . . I have performed four safe deliveries at home for women and one for a goat . . . I also check weight for under-three year old children. For several years now I started a clinic with the help of the government health post worker and we give care to mother and children, do pregnancy tests, see pregnant women, and give iron tablets . . . *So many people believe In Jesus Christ and come to church because of the health teaching . . .*"

---

[54]   Literally, water of life, an oral rehydration solution for replacing electrolytes lost with diarrhea or vomiting.

[55]   VDC or Village Development Committee is the local form of government in Nepal, similar to our municipality.

Kanchi

"I am Kanchi, and I am twenty-six years old, from a small village. I am the eldest daughter of my parents. Before me my mother gave birth to three children, but they all died at a small age. As I am their only daughter, they loved me very much. When I was just seven months old, my right hand was burnt and damaged three of my fingers. When I was eight, my father and mother suffered from a kind of disease. There was no one to care for them, no one to provide them with medicine. I was alone and afraid. Our traditional belief in the witch doctor was practiced in our village. I too had belief on them so I called them, but instead of caring for my parents, they went on demanding sacrifices of virgin goat kids. My entire village was helpless in this critical situation. From that day, I had a life-calling to serving others through health. I never denied helping those who didn't help me before. Even though I didn't know about medicines, I usually carry citamol (acetaminophen) when I went to school. It was very difficult to go to school due to my poor economic condition . . . Ten years ago, I got to know about Jesus Christ. My life was changed, full of joy and happiness. It encouraged me more to my destination, to serve people. I was very busy in my field work and I have to raise my younger brother and sister . . . Then, I went to the crusher factory to crush stone to support my family . . . *Social service was my destination and I was always in the search of it. I prayed to Jesus to show me the way. I got . . . a chance to participate in health training to be a VCHW. I thanked the Lord through my heart.* Then, after that, I started teaching villagers on different diseases like diarrhea, malnutrition, anemia, personal hygiene, etc. Before, no one believed me. Later, I started teaching health to children and youth fellowship. I also started teaching about pregnancy care and newborn care to pregnant women . . . now I am loved by everyone. I thank H.E.L.P with all my heart; whatever I am is due to Christ."

Stories from Traditional Birth Assistants and Maternal and Child Health Workers

P. Sunawar

"My name is P. Sunawar and I live in Okhaldhunga in a very remote area . . . where women are suffering from various problems. I am one of them. Since I believed in Jesus Christ, I care about other sisters who were suffering . . . I was selected to have female community health worker (FCHW) training for eight days. God has blessed me . . . I checked eighteen pregnant women and delivered five. Another I convinced to go to the hospital and helped to collect money for her. *I taught how to and built toilets, clean water sources, and have taught over 80 people in health classes . . . and teach in a woman's group.* Now so much has changed in my village. I have an opportunity to serve in my village as well as the Lord Jesus."

Pasang (story adapted by staff) (Fig 4.3)

During the Maoist conflict, most remote areas had no functional government health posts. Due to strikes and violence, even villages with previous access to medical facilities had none. Pasang, a small, unassuming woman living in the high mountains near Tibet left Buddhism and followed Christ. She had a great desire to serve her people, and through her local fellowship, after learning to read in a H.E.L.P. literacy class, received the opportunity to first be a VHW and then a TBA. Because of her great service in many villages, she became known in surrounding areas. One evening, after successfully assisting in a delivery of a mother and infant, she was approached by a group of Maoist guerillas and held by gunpoint. She was blindfolded, and taken through the jungle for a full day's journey. When her blindfold was removed, she was at a headquarters of the Maoist with hundreds of soldiers, many quite young, and many women. The commander requested that she assist those with medical problems. She did the best she could, relying on prayer more than medication (as she had little). God blessed her and her patients recovered. Three days later her blindfold was replaced, and she was taken back to the village where she had delivered the baby. Her family and our staff was relieved, as all assumed she would never be seen on the earth alive. Pasang has selflessly served as a volunteer health worker with H.E.L.P. for over 12 years.

Som Maya

In 2000, Som Maya was one of our first TBAs trained in a region inaccessible by any vehicle (or road), and near the border of Tibet. I visited her and distinctly remember the hike, as my foot slipped through the broken plank of a suspension bridge, with rapids 1,000 feet below. At that time, she was the only follower of Christ in the area and had been ostracized due to her faith. After becoming a TBA, and proving the love of Christ for her neighbors by her selfless service, she became a leader in health and wellness in the region. Ten years later, Tim happened to be in the same area, and Mrs. Magar, our midwife, explained, "this entire mountain is now inhabited by Christians." One faithful TBA, by providing safe deliveries and childcare to the women of the area, was the light God used to bring His gospel to another area we could never have lived in or assimilated into the culture.

She writes: "My name is Som Maya. I got a chance to take women health worker training organized by H.E.L.P. Before that I had no knowledge about health. After taking the training my eyes opened and realized that we were far back from good health and hygiene. When I took 10 days training at the headquarters and returned to my village, first I started from my own life and family about the cleanness. Then, slowly I started to go out to the neighbor and village. The people used to make fun of me. But still I worked. First I worked with the pregnant women and started to teach them about tetanus, balanced diet and vaccines for children. Before that women never knew we have to take tetanus vaccine during the pregnancy time.[56] I started teaching about uterus prolapse which is common in the village, and how to prevent it.[57] I also taught the bad signs (warning signs) during pregnancy. I also gave health awareness teaching to women, children and everyone in the village. I also taught them how to make sarbotam pitho. The same people who used to hate and tease me believe and respect me and are coming to get advice. Now there is so much change in my village. Now there are toilets for every family also. Time to time Mr. Shah, Mrs. Magar, and Miss Tamang, (H.E.L.P. health staff) come to my village and give health awareness classes. Mr. Prajapati(H.E.L.P. agriculturalist) comes to give us agriculture training. Because of H.E.L.P. literacy program, many people in my village can read and write. Now many people have come to Jesus and it is increasing every day. Now I work among women and children in church ministry too. I teach them about health and hygiene, and causes of disease. I have taken a pregnant lady to the hospital who was about to die (over a day's walk). This is all possible because of God and H.E.L.P. and I would like to give thanks to the Almighty . . ."

---

[56]   Neonatal tetanus is still common due to both lack of immunity in the mother and common practices of delivery of babies in animal sheds and using animal feces on the umbilical cord.

[57]   A condition in which the woman's uterus or womb drops below the level of the vagina, causing pain, infection, and embarrassment. Malnutrition and prolonged labor contribute to this.

Kanta

"My name is Kanta and I live in a village of Chitwan district. I was the most feeling shy person I think in this world. It can be because of my Chaudhary family. In my culture it is not allowed for a daughter in law to go out. Because of that, I was not able to speak the Nepali language well. We have our own Chaudhary language. I had a desire to serve my village but I had no idea how because I had never taken any training or seen anything like that. It was the same with the other women in my village. They never would go to check-up when they became pregnant because they used to feel shy. Due to that, many women used to have miscarriage, some use to have placenta stuck, and some used to have heavy bleeding. There were so many of these kinds of problems. In my whole village there were only toilets by one or two houses. Because of that everywhere beside the path used to be stool and urine. It used to get so bad a smell around the village. Due to that, every time there used to be big problems like dysentery and worms, and many children died. There was so poor cleanness and no hygiene. The children used to walk around never taking bath, never cutting their nails, or washing their hands. Then, I got a chance to take health training organized by H.E.L.P. I heard about it for long time and had great desire to go. One day a sister from the church told me. I was so happy, but a bit hesitant because I could not fluently speak Nepali language. One side I have great desire to learn and serve in my village and the other side is language problem. I was bit confused really what to do. Then, the day came for the training . . . Mrs. Magar asked me, 'Do you want to take the training?' I said yes, and I attended the ten days of training. I learned so many things. I was able to speak better Nepali during my stay too. After I went back home from the training I started teaching both women and the children. I encouraged the pregnant women to go for check-up, even if they felt shy. I also taught them what they should eat and do during pregnancy: about tetanus, taking iron tabs, and about hygiene. I also teach in the village about use of toilets. I encourage them to build toilets and now every house (family) has their own toilet. *After six months of my teaching there is so much changed in children and whole village. Now children known that they should not go to toilet in the road, but in the toilet. Pregnant women go to the health post for check-up. The are much fewer problems during delivery and children are more healthy with good weight. There is big change in my village, my family as well as me. I give a big thanks to the teachers who taught me without feeling bored. Thank you!"*

Indra

"My name is Indra. I was not allowed to go to school . . . but had always wished to. I also wanted to do social work among our women. I got married when I was very young and had children . . . a few years later I received Jesus. Then, I got an opportunity to take the adult literacy class with H.E.L.P. I learned to read and write in Nepali. Later I took health training and the ten-day women health worker training. I went back and first started work with my own home and family. I taught the about health, hygiene, nutrition . . . then I started teaching about health to the neighbors and the community. There was not even one toilet in our village before. Then I called from every house one person and gave the health awareness class and told them why they must have toilet and teach them about pure drinking water and how we will get diseases from unsafe drinking water. I taught them how to purify water. Now there is so much change in our village. I taught the children under five to cut their nails, take bath, and wash their hands before they eat. I give health education to pregnant women and take them to the health post for check-ups, taking iron tablets. Now the pregnant women have safe deliveries. I have done safe deliveries and send women to the clinic who have problems. The women in my village are so happy with me and my work. Every woman comes to my home to get suggestions from me. So many are telling me they want this training too. *Before those who were not talking with me have now started to talk. I am able to teach them about the true God.* I would like to give thanks to our God for opening my eyes . . . and to my teachers."

Mahima

"I am Mahima and I live in a poor village. When I was in class three (third grade) my father said I was learning too much and might write letters to bad boys, so he took me from school. I left home and went to work in a carpet factory in Kathmandu, and then got married. Then . . . I got sick with an evil spirit and used to talk like a crazy person . . . my husband though that I was "mad" and . . . doctors gave me injections and kept me in a room . . . I used to cry, shout, and not let anyone sleep . . . my family used to beat me and in the morning call the witch doctor to do *puja*[58] and all. They used to say that in a few months I would die. They did everything they could like sacrificing goats and chickens, but I didn't get better. One day a lady told me the gospel . . . I realized Jesus is the doctor's doctor, healer, and I prayed and repented and asked forgiveness. In the same night, God gave me a vision. After that I stopped shouting and the evil spirit could not attack me. After 3 days the sister who told me the gospel came to visit me . . . she was so happy and prayed for me. I accepted Jesus as my Savior and grew up day by day . . . I got an opportunity to take Bible

---

[58] Religious ceremonies; in this case, attempts to appease the demons.

training and a pastor asked me, what I would do . . . I will spread the gospel, I said.

. . . When I returned to my village . . . it was very difficult . . . I took health training with H.E.L.P. so I could teach about health and hygiene. I also teach about diarrhea, worms, toilets, and how to build them. I teach women about children's health, malnutrition, family planning. I go to the schools and cut children's hair and nails; I give them education about worms and scabies. After I took the TBA training I have done many safe deliveries, but if I find problems, I send them to the hospital. Sometimes, I even take them to the hospital . . . I am happy because I'm working for God and His people."[59]

Sabitri

"My name is Sabitri and for a long time I have had the desire to work with women. I am a pastor's wife, and go to many villages and women's groups. The women used to share their problems with me, but I didn't know about it either. I only used to pray for them or suggest them to go to the health post. I used to do delivery for four to five women, but didn't know anything about cleanness and hygiene and could not solve the smallest problems. Because of that I had a desire to get more health training. I only got to study to class five, and due to my less education, could not go for more training, but when I asked if I could to take the women's health training with H.E.L.P . . . they said 'yes, the training is for people like you who have not studied much.' I was so happy to hear the news . . . I prayed with God that I can go and take the training. God listened to my prayer and I got an opportunity to take TBA training for ten days. I

[59] Mahima is well-known in the schools, villages, and surrounding areas for her amazing health work. She assists abandoned children and tirelessly labors among the poor.

learned about so many different diseases. I returned back to my village and I'm working with my full heart, with women in the community. I realized that working without learning and with learning makes so much difference. With prayer I give health teaching also. Now among our church members there is so much difference in cleanness and hygiene. Before, they used to get bad smell but now they are taking bath and washing their clothes, looking clean. *Now every woman who has problems in the community is coming to take suggestions from me. First, I teach them about the health and then talk about the gospel."*

Bawana

Bawana came to know Christ out of Hinduism, but was ridiculed by her neighbors. She had just learned to read and write through a H.E.L.P. literacy class at her church, but she had no toilet, and little knowledge of basic health when she came to her ten-day traditional birth assistant (TBA) training. Immediately after her training ended, the very night she arrived home, the husband of a woman in prolonged labor heard she could help, and came to bring her. She responded to his requests, went to the house and did what our nurse midwife and CMA taught her, praying continually; she successfully delivered a healthy baby! Then, the placenta did not deliver, so she again did as taught, put the baby to the mother's breast (for release of oxytocin) and it delivered. Overnight she became the hero of her village. She writes,

"Before taking the training I could not even talk Nepali language, because my language is Newari . . . . Mrs. Magar didi (sister) tried hard to teach me. Whatever I learned during the training I started to share with the women. Before . . . most of the time our family used to get sick. I didn't know the cause of it, . . . but then I learned about health and hygiene . . . I started teaching mothers and sisters how to make sarbotham pitho, about nutrition, vaccines, and prolapsed uterus. Still in my village many sisters have no chance for school. Because of that they don't know many things. Many women were suffering from urine burning, itching and bleeding problems, and they are solved after learning about being clean. I also teach them about cough, fever, diarrhea and how to prevent the sickness. When the mother has a breast infection or abscess, I help them cure. I teach pregnant women and now every woman from my village comes to take advice from me when they are pregnant and sick. When they are sick I take a history first. I also give health teaching and tell why we get sick. I have done many safe deliveries and have sent some to the hospital. After delivery some infants couldn't breathe and I have given artificial oxygen and saved them. In earlier days, many a mother and child used to die due to our lack of education. Not only that, but there was so much lack of cleanness. Now it has changed a lot because I also give health awareness teaching in my church, village, and in my community. Now there is so much change in my village. I'm so happy to teach them and make the difference in their lives. Not only are the changes in the people's lives, but it has made a change in my own life too. I would like to give thanks to God, and to those with H.E.L.P. who taught me."

For over eleven years she has continued to serve her people, sharing Christ, and leading many to saving faith, while saving many other women and children from physical death. Just last year when we met to visit, Bawana said,

"I recently went with a brother (a H.E.L.P. VCHW volunteer) to a village four hours up the mountain. They had never heard of Christ. They are so poor. They have no toilets, no food, no water, and no hope. We must help them. I feel so hungry when I go, because they have no food after I walk there, but we must bring them the gospel, literacy, and teach them about toilets, and how to grow food and . . . ."

Truly she has seen the vision and the true role of health in community development and the spread of the gospel. Starting with her own family, own village, and now her further neighbors, she shares the spirit of Christian community development.

Smokeless Stove (Fig 10.6)

Stories from Participants

Saraswoti

"My name is Saraswoti. H.E.L.P. organized a smokeless stove training in our village through the agriculture group representative. When he taught us how to build one, most of the participants (about thirty) made a smokeless stove in their houses. I also made a smokeless stove in my kitchen. I found a great difference between traditional and improved smokeless stove. We were suffering from smoke that irritated our eyes. We were always 'weeping' when we cook food. We were suffering from headache and cough. We have to smear (mud) walls each day to cover the black stain. The clothes were black and smoky. Now, we are free. There is no black stain inside the room or on clothes. There is no smoky smell in clothes. There is no tear during cooking and not any headache and cough. All the black smoke went out through chimney. Thank you!"

Yumaya

"I am Yumaya. We were using traditional stoves of three stones kept in a pit in the kitchen room. The main problem of that stove is the smoke didn't get out. Nobody is interested to cook food due to smoke. I was suffering from cough and chest ache and was tired from that smoky stove. I got an opportunity to know about the smokeless stove training organized by the farmer group working with H.E.L.P. My daughter came to the training, and then made a smokeless stove in our house. Many neighbors came to watch. Now we have two kinds of smokeless stoves . . . I am pleased with it . . . smoke went outside. I have no cough and food cooked fast. Less firewood is required. What a surprise in my house! Everybody helped me to cook food. My neighbors came to my house requesting smokeless stove in their houses. I shared it to my villagers. Many of my neighbors made a smokeless stove."

R. Bahadur

"You can imagine how old I am by looking at my white beard. I gained different kinds of experience with my white beard. Is it not proved by my wrinkled face? People cooked food in traditional stove in my time. We cooked rice and corn flour called *dhido* in that big stove. Actually, the stove is just a gathering of three big stones. A bundle of firewood is use for cooking food. The whole house is covered with black smoke. This is our tradition, but I did not realize that this is a main cause of different kinds of diseases we were suffering. We have not heard about an improved stove in our time but it is with great pleasure that I can see it with my own eyes . . . . In our time, people covered the house with black smoke to control wood insects. But, I know that it affected our body. So, this new type of smokeless stove is a gift in my old age. How amazing, the black smoke went out. There is also a facility of charcoal stove combined with smokeless stove. It increases the beauty of my home. It is easier to cook food. Now, I am free from black smoke. Therefore, there is decrease in headache and eye irritation. Less firewood is required to cook food. I want to thank the organization that provides this kind of training in my old age. The main benefits I found with this smokeless stove are as follows: no smoke inside the room, less firewood required, no black stain inside the house, no headache and eye irritation, less black stains on the utensils."

Bil (story from Mr. Prajapati, agriculturalist)

"Bil is from a remote village in Sindhupalchowk district. (Fig 6.5) He moved to that village from another, because of poverty and no food. He had a difficult childhood, and hard life. He and his 5 children lived in a small shed provided by the landlord. He became a member of the farmer group started by H.E.L.P. Here he learned many things. He had a traditional stove in his kitchen (open fire) . . . . He received training on a charcoal smokeless stove through a H.E.L.P. training organized by his church. He learned how to make two-sided, one-sided, charcoal, and briquette stove. He made many and sold more than 300 in his village. This became a good source of income for him . . . . Then he could even give to his church . . . He visited another farmer group and learned to make a briquette for the stove from wasted organic materials and red clay soil. Now he makes the briquettes for his village too . . . Now he has plenty of food and can even send his children to school and buy their books."

Agriculture Training

Stories from Farmer Participants (narrated by H.E.L.P. staff, Group Representative, or the farmer)

Mr. Rai

"Mr. Rai was an extremely poor subsistence farmer. He joined the farmer group associated with his village church. His pastor suggested that he take the mushroom training to improve his economic situation, so he came to our training center for a five-day mushroom training. However, as he did not even have the money to buy mushroom spawn (spores) his pastor purchased five bottles for him and another member purchased an iron drum in which he could steam his straw. The church gave him a room to use for mushroom production, and he began work. He made twenty mushroom balls. When I went there for field follow-up the mushrooms were growing well. He even made hanging baskets to keep mushroom balls away from mice. He harvested 1.6 kg mushroom in a single mushroom ball in first picking and a total of 10 kg mushroom on that day. The entire mushroom crop sold to the church members . . . He told me that he will continue mushroom production . . . *He used knowledge and skill learned in training and improved his and his family's health and income.*"

R. Chepang

"R. Chepang is a resident of Makawanpur district. Chepang is a tribe which is known for wandering in the jungle for living. Nowadays, they have started farming. R. is a pastor of local church. He realized agricultural and livestock trainings are required for effective farming.

He contacted H.E.L.P. to provide trainings on agriculture and livestock. The area where he lives is popular for growing marijuana, an illegal crop. Many families do not have enough food as they use their fields only for marijuana. He has a burden to replace that crop with vegetables and livestock. Therefore, he made a farmer group of Christian farmers. He wanted to prove that vegetables and goats provide more benefit than marijuana. It required the collective force and only a farmer group could do it. He organized vegetable and goat training in his church through HE.L.P. He himself took those trainings with other church members. He started to grow vegetables for the first time in his field. He made organic manures using Effective Microorganism (EM). He made "manure tea" from local herbal plants to repel insects. He found the technology we taught him more effective than his earlier practices. In livestock sector, he made improved goat shed and mineral blocks. He is a hard worker and able to coordinate a group wisely. Therefore, we invited him to take training of trainers at our headquarters. After that, we made him a group representative for his area. He is now coordinating four farmer groups of his area. We provided other necessary trainings according to the requirement of his area . . . and he is now teaching hundreds more." *Now there is almost no marijuana grown in his area, the families have more food, and the farmers have more income.*

Sukra

"Sukra took the pesticide and agriculture technology training held at the H.E.L.P. headquarters. He was surprised to know about EM for the first time in his life. He could not believe the various positive impact of EM in agriculture and livestock sector. He decided to experiment in his field so that he purchased one bottle from the organization. He activated EM by mixing with water and molasses. He applied activated EM in cereal crops, vegetable, spice, fruit and livestock. He was so excited he asked us to come to his village and organize a vegetable training. While we were there he invited us to visit his field to see the good impact of EM. At evening after the session, we went to see his field, which is one hour far from the training place. He transplanted a new rice variety in his field. He harvested one kg rice at first and the next year, he transplanted that 1 kg seed and harvested 32 kg rice. This year, he transplanted 12 kg seed and applied EM . . . in his village it is popular to grow illegal crop marijuana, but he refused to plant that crop. He sowed 14 kg ginger instead; this year, he sowed 150 kg ginger seed and applied EM. The plants are greener and production increased more than previous years. He made improved goat shed after he received goat training from H.E.L.P. He found skin-related problems decreased and increased digestive properties of animals. EM also suppressed the foul smell of animal wastes. The manure produced is of high quality."

Bim

"Bim is a member of a farmer group in his village. This group asked to join the agriculture and livestock farmer group association of H.E.L.P. He first came to the headquarters and saw the experimental fields and learned hands-on methods of composting and organic farming. Group representative Kedar . . . prepared a model organic farm in his area and it is not too far from Bim's farm. Bim learned many new practical methods from his farm. Though he could not adopt all the technologies he learnt from Kedar, he did best to adopt them in his farm. He started to prepare organic manures and applied in vegetable farm. His production has increased dramatically."

Kali

"Kali is from Bardiya district. She is the vice president of the local farmer group started by the H.E.L.P. regional GR. She came to the headquarters to receive farmer group conduction training. She was encouraged to see the organic manures prepared in the training center. She was also amazed to see the mushroom cultivation. She was a student in a H.E.L.P. literacy class in her area at that time. She started to counsel with the GR to learn about kitchen gardening.[60] . . . The GR then came to her village and she learned how to sow pumpkin, corn, tomato, and other seasonal vegetables. She prepared manure from local resources. She learned the bad effects of chemical pesticide. She prepared manure tea from local herbs. She made bio-pesticide from urine manure and ash. She started to prepare off-season vegetables in her kitchen garden. She is encouraged to see the vegetables in her kitchen garden. She said, 'I feel comfort to see the production in kitchen garden. We can produce vegetables all year except rainy season.'"

D. Adhikari

"D. Adhikari was the first Christian in his village. He received Jesus Christ before he was 15 years old. At that time, he had to walk more than four hours to reach church in the bazaar. He is physically disabled, so it takes more time for him to walk. Not only the villagers, but even his family members also hated him because of believing in Christ. He had to face a very difficult situation due to his disability and his belief in Christ, but he did not give up. He trusted God and knew God is able to help him. His father died two years after

---

[60] A small plot of land by the home, which provides vegetables primarily for the family consumption.

his believing in God. The villagers and family decided to force him to follow tradition according to Hindu culture . . . he refused. D. described his terrible experience and his thoughts on this occasion.

'My life is not so important as believing in Christ. How can I betray Jesus? I was out of my mind. So, I ran away from village. How much I fell down due to my disabled legs, I do not know. My only target was to reach the bazaar . . . My whole body was covered with mud. My whole body was scratched with thorns and stones. I did not care when my slipper was lost . . . I reached bazaar after more than a five-hour struggle. My pastor hugged me warmly and wept with me. I felt very comfortable in his hug though I was totally ruined.'

Many times the villagers tried to beat him . . . His brothers treated him like a low caste person . . . his wife also hated him. After a few years, he got a teacher job in a local school. The principal warned him not to share the gospel with students. He did not give up sharing the gospel to his students though the principal warned him. I met him for the first time four years ago in vegetable training. He learned happily though his legs made it difficult. He learned many important technologies for farming. He made a charcoal smokeless stove. He planted potatoes and other kinds of vegetables as he had been taught in training. The GR of H.E.L.P. visited his house many times and shared the gospel to his wife. She started behaving positively toward Christianity and also to her husband. His wife accepted Jesus Christ as her Savior when I visited them for the second time. Now he is working in school. His wife helps him in farming. Now, one church is established in his village. The times have changed. *He has proved Christians do hard work in farming and earn a good reputation. Now, villagers do not care about his beliefs though they are reluctant to accept Jesus.* He is happily living with his wife. He became a good farmer by farming with new technologies."

Gopal B.

"The things done by someone in a community gives him an identity that may be good or bad. A community does not like someone with a bad reputation. Similarly, people get respect and honor from a community for his positive impact in a community. Sometimes, someone has fallen in such a way that the community totally rejects him. But, there is always hope even if the community has declared him hopeless. Gopal B. is one of the best proofs that Christ can totally change bad behavior. Gopal lives in Kavre district. He is the father of five children and was a well known drunkard in his village. He could drive a tractor but his alcoholic nature drove him into bad situations. So, he used to take money from his own house to drink alcohol . . . His wife could not commit suicide because she feared for the future of her five children. Gopal was fallen mentally, physically, and socially. He was so mentally disturbed that he burned his house. His family members believed in Christ and hoped he would be healed by Christ because no one else could help him. His family members began taking him to church. Their trust in Christ helped him to heal mentally and physically. Gradually, he became busy in family and social work. Christ totally changed his behavior. He is no longer a drunkard. Slowly, his economic condition began improving. H.E.L.P. introduced him to goat training in 2004 and he began actively participating in that training. He started a goat business which began with five goats and quickly grew to twenty-four goats. He became a model farmer of his region. Now he is busy in his daily agricultural practices. Two of his daughters have married; his son is studying in college and working as a pastor, while his other two daughters are studying in grade 7 and 10." Christ, through the ministries of H.E.L.P. transformed his life.

Binod

"Binod is a Christian; he and his family live in the Chitwan district, in the slum areas. Though he completed grade 10, and had a good house and field, he and his family lost everything but their lives in a landslide. For a year they ate bananas and whatever they could find, and were homeless. He met a GR with H.E.L.P. and decided to use his education to start a literacy class. Next he formed a farmers group and received different kinds of agriculture trainings, after which he organized sustainable agriculture training in his area. He had only a small field, but used what he learned, and shared his skills with his father. His father also began to cultivate vegetables and made beautiful plots from the poor land, but using organic fertilizers. From his training he learned to grow fruit trees, raise chickens, and improved goat sheds for his goats. Another organization was so impressed with his work in the slums that they helped him make a pond for water storage to cultivate vegetables in all seasons. He is teaching all this knowledge to others. H.E.L.P. agriculturalist says, 'We had to cross a river more than five times to follow-up in his fields.'" *With Binod's hard work, the agriculturalist and GR follow-up, and God's blessing, this family now is not just surviving, but thriving and helping hundreds of others in his district who lost their livelihoods and homes through landslides, as well.*

Amar

"Amar is an energetic young man from a remote district. He worked in Malasia for one and a half years, but found himself in a bad situation. He thought he would find easy money there, but returned home, and realized the importance of the agriculture business in Nepal. He actually had to earn money to pay back his loan. He was tired and discouraged. After coming to the farmer field school facilitator training Amar 'became a changed man.' He did research in potato cultivation and found the best manure, using different plots and various treatments. He studies the number of beneficial insects and harmful insects, density of weeds, and plant diseases. He finally decided that EM Bokashi and compost was the best for the potato field. *Now he is organizing a literacy class in his village and teaching more farmers new and sustainable technology. He realizes hard work in his own field produces better results than going to a foreign country to work!"*

K. Shrestha

"My name is K. Shrestha and I live in a village far from the road. I am doing vegetable cultivation and searching for an agriculture technician for advice. I have lots of problems with my vegetables, though I am selling vegetables through my shop. The government technician never came to our village, and when we went to their office, neglected us. One day, one of my neighbors told me to go to another town and visit Netra (GR). She told me he knows many things about agriculture and learning new technology. Netra taught me many new things which I had never heard in my lifetime. He told me about EM, composting, vermicomposting, and manure tea. Because of my thirst for new agriculture technology I often walked the four hours to his village. It is my great pleasure that Netra never hesitated to teach me what he knows. This is the first time I met one special and generous agriculture technician. Then I heard he is a GR for H.E.L.P.[61]

---

[61]   As described above, GRs are group representatives, and are not paid full-time staff. They receive additional training from H.E.L.P. which helps them to earn more income, and gives them skills. Occasionally they are paid a per diem or travel expenses when they assist in trainings, but most of their time is given as volunteers.

He even did soil testing of my field and recommended to me to use more organic manures in my field. So, I started vermiculture in my home. I applied vermi-compost, EM 2, manure "tea", on my potato, cauliflower, radish, cabbage, and tomato vegetables. Amazingly, the vegetables flourished very well. There is now no attack of insect and disease. Among the vegetables, radishes have grown extraordinarily. They are two feet long and weigh up to 9 kg. Now, I am interested in vegetable training so that I can do best in my vegetable cultivation.

Deepak

"My name is Deepak. I work as a church leader in a remote area of Sindhupalchowk. It is difficult for youths like us. Rebels capture us and make us dig their bunkers, explosion tunnels, and arms. So, I have been searching for work. Finally, I found H.E.L.P. could provide me many kinds of agriculture and livestock trainings . . . I made a new goat shed, mineral block, manure, but my father has a traditional mind and smashed my goat shed two times saying it is not right . . . it is difficult to convince the old traditional person . . . I have a burden to change their minds through model farming. H.E.L.P. agriculturalist helped me start a farmer field school in my area and we did experiments on the effectiveness of compost and EM bokashi. I successfully organized mushroom training in my locality with H.E.L.P. and 15 others in my locality also learned to grow mushrooms. Pray for me and for my vision to spread God's kingdom in this remote, cruel area through agriculture and livestock programs. I can answer the rebels that I am engaged in community development!"[62]

---

[62] This testimony was written at the height of the Maoist conflict.

Chandra

"My name is Chandra and I am a member of the local H.E.L.P. farmer group. I am eighteen and want to learn modern farming. Thank God we have a Christian organization to teach us. Last year I got the opportunity to take mushroom training . . . and I have become the pioneer of growing mushrooms in my village. At first, I did not make a profit due to my lack of knowledge . . . GR Sunil came to visit me monthly and advised me on my mushrooms, so now I have produced mushrooms and sell them in my church and village. I have applied modern agricultural technology to my land . . . *and I was able to grow potato and other vegetables through the seed project.*"

J. Mijar

"My name is J. Mijar and I was born in a small farming village. Our main occupation is agriculture, so I spent my childhood in cutting grass and caring for goats. We had no school in our village and education was not in our minds. I married when I was twenty-two . . . we as a couple worked hard in the fields and to care for our goats . . . I had three sons and three daughters . . . we had hoped farming would be easier if we had a large family . . . but the children became a burden and it pressed us to grow more crops. We put more chemical fertilizer and pesticides hoping for more harvest. We felt happy when our fields became green . . . but our happiness did not last long. The grains became shrunken and many new diseases and pests came to our field, the fertility of the soil degraded. It was difficult to send the children to school and the children and livestock became ill due to malnutrition and were suffering from different diseases. We went to see the witch doctors. They demanded a healthy goat, red hen, and *akshyata* (rice grain mixed with a red color) as an offering. We did what they told us, but this increased our debt but neither our children were healed nor our livestock cured. Our life was full of grief and anxiety. We were searching for a solution. At the same time, the pastor of a nearby church came to our house and suggested we participate in the agriculture and livestock technology training organized by his church through H.E.L.P. I was very happy and participated in the training. The local farmer group coordinated the training; I learned many new things in the five days. Most of the knowledge I could use from local resources. I prepared and implemented all these technologies. Now, no more witch doctors are required to heal my children and cure my livestock. At the same training, I accepted Jesus Christ as my Savior. Now am regularly attend a church fellowship . . . I am using organic manure, vermicomposting, other manures, and sell vermicompost. I use mineral blocks to feed my goats and treat my goats . . . villagers are coming to learn about agriculture and livestock technology from me . . . I was selected as the best farmer from my farmer group."

Animal Husbandry

Stories told by a H.E.L.P. Veterinarian Worker or Farmer Participant

M. Thami

"My name is M. Thami. I am from a backward caste which lives by selling bamboo handicrafts and eating forest tubers. I have little land and need to work in landowners land. I have a temporary shed on his land. I got an opportunity to take the goat training through H.E.L.P. I was not a Christian at that time. I was engaged in a civil war in my soul. I received Christ during the goat training and now that war ended. Now my wife, father and mother in law are Christians and we have all joined the farmer group at the local church working with H.E.L.P. I got an opportunity to plant seeds distributed by the seed project. Now I am able to produce seeds and return them back. Extra seeds I will sell and that will be income for me. I got goats from farmer groups and another goat I purchased with a loan from the farmer group. I am providing worm medicine, minerals, and good food to my livestock . . . now I have made a small pond to keep fish . . . *I am keeping livestock though I have no land. Now I sent my wife to the literacy class and she can read the Bible.* The GR helped me sell herbs I collected in the jungle and I gained money to send my children to school. I now know many things about how to use resources around us for income generation. I thank my GR, Om, and my church, our farmer group, and Jesus."

B. Tamang

"B. Tamang is from Nuwakot district. They have five members in the family. Their financial status was very low. It is difficult for them to send their children to a government school. They do not have food to eat for a whole year. They have to work hard on their small farm. They have to work in field as daily worker. Sometime, they get work of carrying luggage in the market. They are searching for an income generation program so that they do not need to wander here and there for food. One day, they heard about poultry training to be held in their church. The pastor encouraged them to participate in the training. Trainers Mr. Ajarya and Mr. Raju taught Mr. Tamang and his wife, Gayung, the management of poultry keeping. They also taught on general diseases and its treatment. She started the poultry business with two hundred chickens in her home. She completed raising five lots of chickens after the training and never suffered financial loss.

She received large net profit in each lot. She is able to treat chickens according to the symptoms seen. Therefore, she thanked trainers and her pastor. She learned many things in management of chickens . . . she keeps the poultry shed clean and dry. She is providing internal and external parasite medicine to the chickens. She learned about poultry shed, temperature management, feed management, water management, application of EM in feed and water, symptoms of diseases. She is providing necessary vaccines to the chickens. Therefore, they are happy to get skill in poultry business. They do not need to worry about food. *She says, 'Now I don't keep animals to survive, but as a business.'"*

Chanarupiya

"I am Chanarupiya. Before this training I didn't know about livestock training. Though we are keeping a few goats in our home, we did not know how to care for them. Many goats and pigs died in our village due to different kinds of diseases. Therefore, if animals started to suffer from disease, we just killed them to eat. I kept animals in traditional way. I did not get good profit from livestock keeping. I was just keeping them for living but not for business. I changed animal keeping after the training. I knew the benefit of improved goat shed . . . different scientific technologies that keep animals healthier than traditional methods. I knew now the importance of ventilation in goat shed . . . about mineral block, mineral bolus, balanced feed, EM, internal parasite medication, breed improvement and importance of legumes and non-legumes grasses. The goat weight reached less than 10 kg before the training but now, the weight increases up to 25 kg. The goats gave birth twice a year. Therefore, I want to thank the organization and the trainers."

G. Rai

"G. Rai is from Khotang district. He received goat keeping training held in his village. He was keeping goats in a traditional way before he received goat keeping training. They used he-goat for breeding to sacrifice to gods. Therefore, the goat breeding process was totally traditional. There was a lack of breed improvement. He learned about medication and goat shed management after the training. Before . . . the goats died after suffering from diseases and they could not get profit. After training and follow-up he made improved goat shed and started breed improvement. Goats were healthier than before, therefore, income from goats increased. He is happy with the training. He said,

'Sir, we are living in remote area. You may know how it is difficult to reach this village . . . you have to change many buses and have to walk to cross the suspension bridge. We have no bridge over Sunkoshi and Dudhkoshi River. Therefore, the cost of living is very high. The prices of commodities are double to triple from its original price. We are living behind the modern technologies. Raju sir came for training. At that time, we are so much happy that we have no words to share our happiness. Now, you came for vegetable training. We are overwhelmed with joy. H.E.L.P. organization is formed for remote underprivileged villagers like us. I made goat shed and it helps to keep clean the shed. Goats are healthier. I started to feed balance grasses including legumes and non-legumes. Thanks for our Lord who sent His children to meet with us and train us in different technologies.'"

Chadamani

"Chadamani is an experienced farmer. Previously, he was a troublemaker and gambler, but met Christ through the witness of his brother, the first to become a Christian in their family. He is member of a H.E.L.P. farmer group associated with his church. Before, he applied lots of chemical fertilizer and pesticides to his farm. Once, however, he became very ill from inhaling pesticides. When he began searching for alternative technology, he received a book by H.E.L.P. agriculturalist (in Nepali) about new ways to farm organically. He had the opportunity to take the fruit cultivation training offered in his village, and learned so much, that he became a trainee of one of the farmer field schools of H.E.L.P. Over the next two years, he learned more methods of organically growing crops, received training in many types of effective microorganism, and implemented a system of rice intensification. He also made vermicompost and became a GR for H.E.L.P., teaching others both near his home, and in villages up to a day's walk or bus ride away." As he teaches farmers how to crow more crops safely, he also shares the good news of Christ, and encourages brothers and sisters to remain faithful.

Shiv

Shiv is a young man living in a remote, mountainous village. He states,

"I had a great desire to take livestock training and start a business, but I had too many obstacles and too many problems at home to go study somewhere. When I heard from my church that H.E.L.P. was having a goat training in the nearby village, I wanted to grab the opportunity. I learned many things during that 7 days; I changed my goat shed and learned what to feed and how to treat my goats. My neighbors began coming to me for advice, when they saw my success. Through this training, I met the H.E.L.P. livestock technician and also learned from him about care of buffaloes and other domestic animals. He helped me to start a livestock service center in my small home and I can buy medicines from H.E.L.P. for a reasonable price."

Prem and Kristina

"Pastor Prem and his wife Kristina live in a remote hilly district where transportation facilities are very poor. Recently construction on a road began, but there is no bridge connecting their village even to that road. Prem spends much of his time as a pastor, so Kristina has more responsibility for the farming. Her daughter also helps her, and as she is more educated, she attended the H.E.L.P. goat keeping training. Then, her daughter taught the family what she had learned. Kristina learned about improved goat shed and breed improvement from her daughter. She did not forget the comment from her trainer, that her goats were 'chicken goat.' Truly her goats were not taller than a cock. This was happening because her goats were not flourishing due to improper breeding, keeping on the wet ground, and nutritional problems. Within one year she sold her goat for ten times the price from the year before, and people came from across the river to breed with her goat. She was so encouraged with the training so that, she sent her daughter to vegetable training held in her church, to likewise improve her production of vegetables!"

Sirku

"Sirku lives near Trisuli. He has minimal education and agriculture production is his main occupation. Farming production provides only three to four months' food for his family. He needs to work as a daily wage workers the other months, therefore, his life is very hard. There are five members in his family and all of them depend upon him . . . farming could not eliminate the hunger of his family members. The farming practices he used were also traditional. He was searching for new technologies to use in the farm . . . he was excited when his pastor informed the church about our poultry training. He said, 'I am very much happy with this skill-oriented training. I started a poultry business from one hundred and fifty chickens and got a net profit (of $150) in my first attempt. Therefore, I am much encouraged. I want the thank the Lord and the trainers. Now I am keeping four hundred chickens.' He now is self-employed and does not worry about food for living. He also gives offerings for his church. He is now able to treat chickens due to his training and experience."

Proof of Success

Several years ago, as we were compiling hundreds of stories from individuals all over the Himalayan region, we were approached by a large donor asking for "concrete" evidence of H.E.L.P.'s success in economic generation and changed lives. Quoting other much larger, better funded organizations, he requested before and after data surveys, detailed numbers, and statistics confirming that we were truly making a difference. Though these would be helpful and exciting to see, it is important for donors to recognize that a truly community-based movement takes years to develop and is hard to quantify in these terms. In order to perform surveys of any validity, trust and understanding of the local people is a necessity. Many surveys are inaccurate as villagers are suspicious of outsiders and will not give information accurately. These surveys are often completely false, as improvement in production of a given crop or in literacy rates must be seen for the donations to continue, thus encouraging false reporting.

Even statistics on health are affected by the lack of birth and death statistics, and lack of trust in those surveying. Because we have not had the luxury of personnel or the means to conduct pre- and post-intervention surveys, we must trust firsthand information we get from site visits, overall statistics from areas in which we work, and the hundreds of families we meet whose lives have been transformed. The stories above we have translated and printed are only a handful of over 500 written testimonies (and thousands unwritten), verified by us, our staff, our GR's and local leaders. Our prayer is that as long as H.E.L.P. is accomplishing God's work, He will provide finances to accomplish the outreaches that take money to do so!

Biblical Principles

1. *In sustainable Christian community development, both the principles of discipleship and the motive of love are critical.* Those whose lives have been truly transformed by the love of Christ desire to help their neighbors, and reach out to help others in their own and nearby communities who are in need.

   "If anyone has material possessions and sees his brother in need but has no pity on him, how can the love of God be in him? Dear children, let us not love with words or tongue but with actions and in truth." IJohn 3:17,18

2. *As is obvious in these testimonies, both the giver and the receiver of Christian community development is blessed in his deeds.* ". . . the Lord Jesus himself said, It is more blessed to give than to receive." Acts 20:35

Chapter 9

An Orphanage and Foster Care

A Different Plan

Tim and I have always loved children, and nothing draws the heartstrings of our compassion more deeply than seeing destitute children. Many of these little ones, through no fault of their own, are suffering from lack of simple food, clothes, and shelter. As the Maoist insurgency in Nepal worsened, the already growing number of street children in our area skyrocketed. The government, NGOs, and INGOs ran a handful of homes for orphaned or abandoned children, but many were full, without funding, or without the healing ministry of the gospel. In our area there was one well-funded agency, but a poor child with no connections could not hope to be admitted. Tragically, many of these abandoned children had a living parent who either did not, or could not, care for them. Our community had its share of prostitution, alcoholism, and mental illness. We hoped that as we improved sanitation, nutrition, and economics, community health would improve and fewer children would be orphaned or abandoned. While progress was being made, however, we realized that true sustainable development takes time. With the added economic and social stresses of the revolution, the situation for the nearly 40 percent of the population under age eighteen grew more dismal daily.

God, in his sovereignty, had a different plan from ours. The teaching hospital where I served on medical school faculty was located off a busy road in a larger town about five miles from our home. Riding my bicycle down the trash-laden roads, I saw crowds of little boys congregated around the bus stop.

Older boys frequently worked at roadside tea shops—dirty, open outdoor fires with a small roof overhead where passers-by could grab a cup of tea and a biscuit. Each day I noticed two little boys poorly dressed

> **At H.E.L.P., our focus was on developing communities in such a way that they could care for those in need; we had no intention of beginning any sort of children's outreach or orphanage.**

and hungry. The older, Ram (about seven years old) busily served at the tea shop, but his brother, Laxman (about four years old), regularly came to beg from me or any sympathetic-looking face that happened to approach him. I inquired about their family and found that their mother was mentally ill and their father was dead; they wandered the streets. Our friendship grew, and I asked a local shop to provide them food daily, at my cost.

Meanwhile, a close physician friend living in this town decided to reach out to the women who were abandoned or widowed during this national time of crisis, in an attempt to rescue them from prostitution and poverty. Shortly after God gave her this vision, she was diagnosed with cancer; as her health plummeted and she needed some assistance, I agreed to help her with outreach to these women. Within a week, it was obvious that in addition to these ladies, there were a growing number of little boys (ages four to ten) showing up at the shelter looking for food. Many families in remote areas were sending their children away, out of fear that they could be drafted into the Maoist armies, or because of inability to feed them after the loss of farms, property, or life. We noticed the growing number of these children on the streets, and there were no easy answers. Most families could not afford to take on another child and many of these boys were not from the best backgrounds. As we began praying about this, God began to bring these children to my mind constantly. Every night I cried myself to sleep as I thought of so many children who—unlike my four—had no food, no love, no home, and no knowledge of the Savior. At the same time, H.E.L.P. work was expanding and we had nearly exhausted our personal savings. In addition, we had seen a decrease in donations since we were not able to return to the United States to keep supporters informed of the work. We simply had no money and no promise of more coming!

We met with community leaders, pastors, and our H.E.L.P. staff and asked whether we should consider opening a children's home. After visiting some well-established orphanages, talking with others who had tried (or given up on) such endeavors, we felt God said there was no choice. I had previously cared for the medical needs of children in some Christian orphanages, and had held long conversations about the difficult realities of institutional rearing of children. Retrospectively, had we realized the difficulty, pain, and responsibility we were undertaking—not to mention the huge financial responsibility—we probably would have never embarked on this chapter of our adventure. While the vision of Christian community development included teaching nationals to care for the less fortunate and vulnerable of their community, we had no desire to begin an institution or do for them what we felt they could do themselves. Some of the more mature believers and churches *did* see the need for this ministry, but the financial needs were overwhelming for them to undertake it alone. Trusting that God would care for these children, we gathered the money we had and plunged into a new area of life.

Beginning with a tiny apartment, six boys, and a house mother, we initially opened a small home for the neediest boys and girls. Some had a mother who was a prostitute, some had no mother or father, and others did not know if their parents were alive or dead. Within a month, we realized the need to move to a cleaner location, so we rented the building next door to the Badals, one of the two pastors in the town where we lived. Mr. Badal recommended a couple from his church, who claimed to share our burden to help these children. We later hired a couple (on the recommendation of another pastor in a nearby town) to assist with teaching and tutoring these children who needed extra help to succeed academically.

Over the next year, *Jyoti Niwas* (House of Light) grew exponentially. (Fig 8.1-8.6) Through the network of H.E.L.P. trainings, word spread that a desperately needy orphaned or abandoned child could be accepted to our home without any "connections." Local Hindus and Buddhists, as well, were thankful that we were reaching out to help these children. In fact, we later realized that though our community work had a deeper and longer-lasting impact, the compassionate ministry to the children was critical in our acceptance as a beneficial NGO in the community and area. During this time, Tim and I invested huge amounts of energy in getting to know and teaching the children. Each of our own four children developed friendships with them, taught them to read, played soccer with them, and invited all of them to every birthday party. (Fig 3.4) In fact, two boys later admitted into Jyoti Niwas were playing in the street when they heard the noise from Aaron and Austin's party, and came to see what was so fun.

Most of our children had medical problems. When examining him on his admission physical, Umesh clearly had physical findings of congenital heart disease. Through God's provision, we were able to afford to have him evaluated and treated as one of the early cases of heart surgery performed by a Nepali surgeon (United States-trained). Another boy from a distant village, Raj, was left with us by his neighbor who had attended a H.E.L.P. training. She anticipated that he would lose his leg—he'd had oozing wounds for at least a year. He had begged from house to house and had minimal food, love, or care. After two weeks of antibiotics, cleaning, good nutrition, and love, his legs healed completely, but he was permanently deaf in one ear from chronic ear infections and a perforated eardrum.

Naresh's grandmother never told us she had leprosy; a compassionate Christian woman brought him to us. His mother, only thirteen years old and nowhere to be found, was forced to marry and became pregnant shortly after. She was abandoned by her drug-abusing husband. Naresh developed full-blown leprosy and transmitted it to two other children. Other children arrived with undiagnosed hemophilia, anemia, tuberculosis, end-stage liver disease, and many other conditions. Virtually all were malnourished when they arrived, and we counted the number of roundworms passed after de-worming new arrivals. Most tragic, however, was the abuse and neglect all the children had suffered.

As we prayed and worked to have a home that was truly a place of healing and light, we began introducing non-traditional ideas. We began a choir and offered music lessons, art, card-making, and more creative activities. A local school with a Christian principal was opening, and the school promised to work closely with us to provide the best education to the children. Central to the belief in reincarnation is the idea that *karma* results from the good or bad deeds of your previous life. These children, in the minds of many of the less educated villagers, were simply suffering for their sins in a previous life, and thus deserved their misery. In our community, however, people of all religious backgrounds were supportive of the work, and those from local churches brought food and donations as they were able.

Every Child Has a Story

Each child admitted to Jyoti Niwas has a story. Samjana was brought by a pastor and his wife. She was about four, and already was being beaten regularly. After her father's death, her mother married another man as his second wife. Two days after marriage, she abandoned Samjana and the new step-father, stealing his money. For years Samjana struggled with emotional and behavioral issues, but today she is a new creation in Christ Jesus, a beautiful young lady who leads the little girls in Jyoti Niwas. Sanju and Suman were sitting by a roadside covered with dirt when a kind man found them. Through village officials we found that their father had left for India and there were no relatives. Because we were one of few homes allowing boys and girls, we were able to keep the siblings together. Today they are close, and they have each other and their faith in Christ. Both are sweet, intelligent children, a testimony to the love of the Nepalese who care for them. Laxman, the friendly beggar who was an inspiration to start Jyoti Niwas, came as soon as he found he could get free food; however, when I asked his brother Ram Kumar if he wanted a home, the tea shop owner where he worked (illegally) told me he did not want to come. As I did not realize she was lying, we did not encourage him; at least he had shelter and food, and she seemed to care for him. God used a nearly disastrous calamity to bring him, as well.

After outgrowing the small apartment and preparing to move down the road to a new location, I had noticed that the flat roof in our soon-to-be-occupied home had no ledge; a child could easily fall off of the top of the third story. I informed our house parents that prior to the children moving to the building, we had to employ a bricklayer to place a wall around the edge, and not allow any children on the roof. The day before the move, I dreamed that Laxman fell off the roof, and the next morning, again told the Jyoti Niwas staff to be sure to have the wall built before the children moved in the house. I did not share my dream, assuming it was just a manifestation of my anxiety about the children in general. Twenty-four hours later, I received a call from the house mother, who was screaming: "Laxman fell off the roof, and I don't know what to do!" I ran over to the home and found Laxman moaning, but alert. Amazingly, after I had fully examined him, we discovered that he survived the three-story fall with nothing more than a kidney contusion (from which he recovered quickly) and some bruises. Incidentally, the bricklayer had fallen ill that day and did not come to lay the bricks and build the wall. Laxman had disobeyed, run up to the roof, and fallen off. This was one of many miracles in which God protected us from harm to the children and closure of our home; an investigation into the event would have likely been the end of Jyoti Niwas. When we brought Laxman to the hospital, I begged Ram Kumar to come see him, initially not sure of the extent of his injuries. Leaning over his bed, looking into his little brother's eyes, and seeing our love for him, he said, "Auntie, I will come." He never tried to run away, immediately adapted to the environment of the home, and became one of our best and smartest boys.

Another sibling pair, Biroj and Romi, arrived a few months later. Their mother had left an abusive, alcoholic husband. She came to saving faith in Christ and was living in a church in Kathmandu with four-year-old Romi. Biroj had run away from home several years before and had been living on the street. His mother knew he was alive, but had no idea where or how he was living. At ten years of age, he was unreachable and, by most statistics, too far gone to ever adapt to living in a home. His mother and the elders of her church did not give up, and when they heard of Jyoti Niwas, called us. The children's mother suffered from primary pulmonary hypertension, a condition from which she was expected to die within a period of months. When we met, she wept and shared with me, "Didi (big sister), my dying request is that my children can grow up to know Christ, as I do."

Through a series of miracles, intense prayer, and hard work on the part of Nepali believers, we were able to find Biroj. When he finally arrived in response to the pleas of his dying mother, we noticed his ill appearance. He was burning with fever and in pain from infection with *salmonella typhi*.[63] I admitted him to the hospital and began antibiotics. Had the timing been different, he would not have survived. Overall, Biroj did amazingly well, attending school and studying. He developed athletically and was one of the top soccer players and athletes in our area of Nepal, competing at a national level. Though Biroj did lead a little troupe of boys to run away a year later (only to return when they got hungry), when the house parents prayed with him and counseled him he reaffirmed his commitment to "take care of my sister." Against all odds and despite the "freedom" he had experienced on the street, Biroj stayed and graduated from high school, learning to sing and play guitar to honor his promise to his mother, his love for his sister, and his love for Christ. Last year he composed a beautiful song about his journey from being a street boy to knowing Christ; he is a talented young singer and guitar player who loves the Lord, but is still a bit of a free spirit!

Umesh, who had the heart surgery, and his little sister, Usha, were brought by their aunt and uncle, who could not even care for their own children and did not want additional mouths to feed. Their father had died, and their mother left them and remarried. Miraculously, after eight years, their stepfather and mother came to Christ, located

---

[63]   *Salmonella typhi*, the causative bacteria of typhoid fever, is contracted from contaminated food or water in unclean (fecally contaminated) environments. It is a common cause of death in the developing world.

the children, and have taken over the responsibility of rearing Usha. Umesh, a young man, is pursuing higher education, training as a pastoral assistant in his village, and helping his family. Usha is now in the Jyoti Jiwan program as her parents could not afford her school fees for highschool, and she regularly comes to the reunions at Jyoti Niwas to see her "other family."

At a bus stop next to the road in a nearby district we frequented, we noticed a deaf and mute woman with a young boy selling bits of fruit and begging. Our CMA, Mr. Shah, told me that he thought she was pregnant a result of rape. As we were in the area once every month or two and worked with the church in her village, we offered to have the local TBA and our health team assist her at the time of her delivery. Unfortunately, it was monsoon season and the road closed due to a landslide. During the ensuing weeks she delivered the baby and died shortly after. God laid both the baby and her other child on my heart, and though we had just left Nepal, we frequently contacted and asked the staff to try to locate and ensure the well-being of the children. Prior to his birth, while praying, God gave me a name for the baby: Samuel (called of God.) Finally, nearly eight months later, Tim was traveling through the same village on his first visit back to Nepal after six months in the United States. He and the health team found the older boy, Umesh N., in terrible condition with no one caring for him. They also discovered baby Samuel in the dilapidated bamboo shack of his presumed father; he had a broken leg (femur) and was severely malnourished. Tim insisted we transport the child back to the hospital, but the "father" refused, asking for money. One of many reasons we had turned all day-to-day activities over to locals was the expectation (created by both aid organizations and even Christian mission organizations) of handouts from "rich" Americans. Now, again, this was a hindrance. Thankfully, through the support of the local community leaders who saw the mistreatment of the child and knew our health team, we were able to get medical care for Samuel. We also brought his half-brother, Umesh N., an acrobatic and intelligent child who had learned to survive by entertaining passers-by, to Jyoti Niwas. Both boys have become wonderful children. Perhaps more miraculous, Samuel's father recently came to Christ, and has been in contact with Samuel. Though he is still desperately poor, he is learning to grow crops and improve his physical and spiritual condition through H.E.L.P. ministry and encouragement from fellow believers. He has even requested that both boys be his adopted sons when they reach the age to leave Jyoti Niwas. Only the power of Christ can rescue the fatherless and give them a father in such a miraculous way.

Jyoti Jiwan

As God brought more and more of these children, we realized that Jyoti Niwas could not house all the children who needed help (as we had no money to care for them) and that the local communities and families needed to take more responsibility for the needy in their area. After much prayer and brainstorming, I suggested the possibility of foster care. The pastors and church leaders strongly discouraged me, saying that in their culture, with the caste system, it could not work. The only alternative, they suggested, might be assisting a family member who could not otherwise afford to care for an additional child (niece, nephew, cousin, etc.) without extra income or food.

In 2003 we started the *Jyoti Jiwan* (Light of Life) program. Through this program, H.E.L.P. worked with a local church to provide one meal a day and the cost of government school and supplies to children of a single parent, grandparent, or relative of an orphan. We required the supervision of a local accountability partner (someone to give us receipts and check on the family), as well as one of our staff, to make sure food, books, school tuition, and similar items actually got to the child. We had to stop expanding this program; in remote villages, it was quite difficult to obtain receipts and ensure that children received the benefits. However, as H.E.L.P. development expanded to some of the poorest of the poor in 2013, the need to assist children like these became more urgent. Utilizing our GRs, we changed the program and now personally provide the books, backpacks, and tuition so that no cash money exchanges hands. The GRs provide follow up, and each year we provide teaching and games for the children and their caretakers. Our prayer is that this will be expanded in the future to include more training for the families, and that the economic benefits of our agriculture and animal husbandry program will give these families the means to care for the children on their own without any monetary assistance from us.

Despite the difficulties of managing Jyoti Jiwan, God has blessed many children through this program, and continues to bless more. Chandra, our first boy, was in class six when his grandmother requested assistance through her village church, and one of our agriculturalists had been in the village and knew the needs. He was orphaned, but she cared for him and was able to pay for uniforms, books, and fees until class six, when they increased. He was supported through the Jyoti Jiwan program at a cost of less than ten dollars a month, passed his SLC exam, continued on to class twelve, and is now well employed and supporting his community and family, as well as serving the Lord. Had he been sent to the city to work at age thirteen, he likely would have fallen into bad company, and never returned to his village. Mina, only seven when her mother died, needed some food and basic needs. Her father applied for help, but after three years of support through Jyoti Jiwan, when he was able to produce more crops, he thanked us, and informed the GR that he no longer needed help with Mina: we should help someone else more needy!

A new opportunity arose several years after we initially considered—and rejected—the idea of foster care. Our policy for Jyoti Niwas and Jyoti Jiwan usually requires children to have been abandoned, have no living parents, or have a handicapped or desperately poor single parent. Some of the highest risk children, however, have a father or parent capable of caring for them but who is *not* caring for them. Some fathers are migrant workers who live in temporary shelters, or hunt animals in the jungle for a living. This leaves the boys to get into trouble on the street and ensures a future of hopelessness and poverty. At the time, a local pastor with a compassionate heart who was serving on the local Jyoti Niwas board told us of five boys who had a living parent incapable of feeding, clothing, and rearing them. He was willing, but did not have enough funds to care for these boys. This situation fit our ideal development path. Jyoti Niwas already had forty-four children and was overcrowded; a larger institution wasn't the answer. Fostering would provide more individual attention for these boys. *Asha House* (House of Hope) was similar to the concept foster care we had once rejected, but it came six years later and suggested by one of the very pastors who thought foster care would not work!

Unfortunately, though all the children had heartbreaking stories, discovering *which of these stories were true* proved harder than we ever dreamed! For example, a kind Christian woman found Tej and Sheer under a bench in a big city and brought them to us. Nearly a year later, we found a relative of theirs, and discovered that they had a mother and stepfather who were willing to take them; they had actually run away! Esther had a tragic story of abandonment, but a year after she came, her extended family insisted on taking her to see her "dying grandmother"; she never returned. Her documents were falsified and we found her mother was alive. Though we did not like her living situation, there was nothing we could legally do. In other cases, we found that families hired agents to look for orphanages so their child would receive care and education for free. These agents would provide "official" documents, death certificates, and verification of the sort required. At a convenient time, or after the child completed his school, the parents reappeared to claim the child. Children were coached in what to say, and they were convincing actors and actresses. All of these obstacles, enough to fill another book, made it much more difficult that we anticipated fulfilling our good intentions of caring for destitute children. By working with local officials, other orphanages, and a consortium of children's homes, these problems have slowly decreased over time, but it is still difficult to help the most needy children.

When we returned to the United States, we left behind a group of dedicated Nepalese making most of the decisions about Jyoti Niwas. However, they did not know all the regulations, and the regulations were changing. As we were already in the process of applying for NGO status, inadvertently delayed by the Maoist problems and purposely delayed by our own "Judas" (see below), we decided to make the children's home an extension of the NGO, so that any other ministries to children could also be within that organization. As required by law, the NGO board would then govern the staff and day-to-day activities of Jyoti Niwas, as well as all the branches of H.E.L.P. These administrative decisions and the whole process would have never been possible without Mr. Bajrachara, our accountant and administrator who had supervised the building of *Manthano*, knew everyone in the area, and seemed able to do almost everything!

Currently, the NGO board has the final decision responsibility of evaluating applications to all of our children's programs, both Jyoti

Niwas and Jyoti Jiwan, verifying the truth of the child's situation (usually by actual visits or references from community members they know), and enforcing the day-to-day rules. Tim and I, as well as the U.S.-based non-profit H.E.L.P. board, act more as initial visionaries (though our Nepali colleagues often have vision or build on that which God gives us), give the final okay to requests for children, and pray. GRs play a critical role, as do literacy facilitators, in finding the neediest children and evaluating who can safely stay in the village, and who needs to come to the home. With the recent changes and geographic expansion of Jyoti Jiwan, GRs have the critical role of following up on these children.

Orphans Coming of Age

One issue we did not consider is that cute children grow into teenagers and then adults. I felt strongly that we should not separate siblings, so we had both teenage girls and boys living in the Jyoti Niwas. These teens had been abandoned and mistreated, making them even more vulnerable to need for love and attention. In addition, we lived in a culture in which the parents arrange the marriages for the children. Some of our children had an uncle or aunt who might be involved in their lives, but others had no one. Where would they find a husband or wife? Where could they find jobs? With a dismal employment rate in the cities and no land or family support for subsistence farming (the most common job for a Nepali), what could we do to help the children become independent? Government regulations demanded that children leave the home at eighteen years of age, but some of our kids started school at age ten! As we searched for ideas and talked with other orphanages, we learned that almost none had vocational training plans and only a few had funding for higher education. This left many children from homes around the country to return to the streets as teens, destined for a life of drug abuse and crime.

To avoid this, we began our first steps toward vocational training with an agricultural program called "friendship with nature." Mr. Prajapati taught the children how to manage our fields at the training center (also the Jyoti Niwas home), while Mr. Raju taught them how to care for the livestock. Through games and activities they learned about "good" and "bad" insects, organic pesticides, composting, and the best methods to utilize manure. Some cows and goats were donated by neighbors and the children cared for them, as well. We had casualties among the livestock, but the children learned, and we also observed which of the children had skills in certain areas of veterinary and agriculture work.

In school, older children tutored younger ones. As we identified some who were nearing 18 years but struggled academically, we began to teach them other trades, recognizing that higher education would not be feasible. When both our US and Nepali boards decided to purchase an additional piece of land down the road from Jyoti Niwas, and God provided the funds in order to have a training center separate from the orphanage, we used the opportunity to teach the older boys about construction and bricklaying. We paid them for their work, and then Mr. Bajracharya taught them how to open a bank account and save their earnings. Mushrooms, a highly nutritious cash crop, provided a means to improve our food supply and teach the children to grow food and earn money. We even invited children from other orphanages to participate in mushroom and candle-making training led by our staff. Several older boys and girls were interested in floriculture, so we sent them to a government-sponsored training, and they began a small floriculture center in our headquarters. Two of our older boys, skilled in raising livestock, began a small poultry farm (under supervision of the animal husbandry department) to provide income and food for the children. Soon, the cows donated by generous neighbors produced enough milk for the children to drink and to collect and carry milk to the market to sell.

Binoj, one of our older Jyoti Niwas boys, was interested in health and began helping Mrs. Magar check his younger siblings' height and weight and assisted in trainings; through a sponsor, H.E.L.P. paid for him to attend school and become a CMA. Raju, another one of the boys, began traveling with Mr. Prajapati, assisting him in teaching farmers new agriculture techniques. He also oversaw the crops with the younger children. Also through a donor sponsorship, he was able to go to a government school after class ten, for further certification as an agriculture technician, to continue working with us. Muna and Ruben scored well in their SLC exams and went on for veterinary technician and health assistant school, respectively. Asmita had a dream to become a nurse, and through generous sponsorship she is now enrolled in a college. Himani, a beautiful young lady who as a young girl was barely surviving in a goat shed, has passed her SLC, completed bakery training and is now in hotel management school. All of these young people (and more) are able to study through the sponsorship of generous individuals and/or churches. They look forward to being able to both provide for their own needs and give back to H.E.L.P. as staff or as donors, assisting other children like themselves. Many of them have been, and continue to be discipled and mentored by older staff of H.E.L.P. Currently we have three junior staff who, after their two year contract, may either stay with the organization, or go elsewhere to serve God and their community.

Since some of the children who came to Jyoti Niwas began school late, they quickly became too old to stay in our home. Foreseeing this problem, we explored options with the education department and began an "open school," which allows a work-study program. This has been highly successful. Many of the children now in higher education even completed class ten in the "open school." Some of the children with special health issues or handicaps have also had unique needs. Bikash, who has hemophilia, took floriculture training and was able to work in a nursery. Ramesh, who has Wilson's disease[64] will need vocational training. Urmilla had some learning difficulties, but is wonderful in her care of livestock and farming; she has received additional training in sewing, as well. Our current house parents, a talented retired pastor and his wife, have vision to continue much of the income generation and training our children have growing up in Jyoti Niwas—caring for animals, crops, selling milk from the cows, sewing, making candles, and more. In addition we continue to include a focus on daily devotions, art, music, and singing, all designed to heal and prepare these children for the future. Many of these creative ideas, as well as many others, were developed by H.E.L.P.'s national director, Mrs. Bajracharya, who in spite of her busy position with all the departments, has a mother's love for the children and oversees and encourages the Jyoti Niwas staff, as well.

> **Though Jyoti Niwas continues to grow and has produced some of our upcoming full-time staff and leaders in the church, the real future of ministry to orphans and abandoned children belongs to the local church. Outside money and foreigners can never effectively meet these needs; Christian community development can.**

We continue to search for new and innovative ways to develop the skills of the children as they come of age. Though we have involved children from other homes in some specific trainings, we have not yet begun a full-fledged program for needy children outside of our

---

[64] A hereditary condition which leads to liver failure, if not recognized early and treated.

programs who do not have those same opportunities. Perhaps God will open that door in the future, and we can have a full-fledged vocational training program, similar in many ways to our community development program, designed for teenagers who do not have the support of their own family.

Because of financial stresses, as well as the emotional issues of caring for children and having them for life, we have on many occasions asked the Lord to allow us to phase out Jyoti Niwas. Instead, at this time, He has directed us to shift our focus more to girls, and to expand the Jyoti Jiwan program (see above). Although literacy and income generation, hand in hand with the transformational power of the gospel, are by far the most effective weapons against prostitution of young girls, we often did not have orphaned or abandoned girls referred to us. Instead, they are taken into homes and treated as virtual slaves or, when old enough, sent to brothels. Recently God has been sending us little girls, and we believe as long as He provides the means to care for them, we will do so, though we are not excluding boys.

Christian community development reduces the number of orphans by improving health, hygiene, and nutrition of parents. It teaches the morality of God's word and provides an economic alternative to combat the sex trade, and it educates and empowers women. By focusing on the root causes and including men, we witness family stability and longer lasting impact. Economic development gives families and communities income with which they can care for their own as well as provide for relatives or neighbors in need. We have witnessed community transformation, as well as personal transformation, as believers in Christ grow in their faith and in their compassion for those less fortunate.

Tika and I became friends in 2000 when she was one of our first TBAs. When visiting with her in 2011, I asked her about a young boy in her home. "You know, all of my boys died, and my daughters are grown. This is my cousin's son. He is an orphan now. I thought, why should I send him to Jyoti Niwas, when I can care for him?" Tika has learned through H.E.L.P. indigenous missionaries, literacy facilitators, agriculturalists, and a nurse midwife, how to read and write, grow crops, cook food with her smokeless stove, raise bees for honey, and safely deliver babies (over 50 to date). But more important, she *now understands her own responsibility as God has blessed her.* Truly, we can empower nationals to care for their own vulnerable and needy, rather than encouraging them to depend on outside sources for those needs.

Abandoned Old Folks

Though also not in our initial plans, one of the pastors with whom H.E.L.P. works felt called by God to begin a home for abandoned elderly. In 2000, when we found a demented, homeless woman living in filth and poverty near our home, he welcomed her to join two other elderly women into his "Old Folks Home". In spite of her mental instability (which caused her family to throw her out), she was welcomed in love. She was joined by other elderly men and women deformed by leprosy, riddled with arthritis, and crippled by accidents; though rejected by their families because of physical or mental handicaps, they were and are loved and cared for by a community of believers. Their bedrooms are rooms for Bible study on Sunday. Despite physical and mental handicaps, they do whatever work they can do, serving the hundreds who attended services and Bible studies by cutting up vegetables or

> Rather than building an institution, Christian community development and the economic freedom it brings enables the indigenous Christian community to reach out to their own families, and then to others in the community, to meet the needs of the vulnerable.

217

helping around the property. Though this church has provided for many of the needs, H.E.L.P. contributes generously to this ministry. It is a blessing to join with other brothers and sisters to help those despised and rejected by the world. This ministry of compassion is a testimony and has caused many of other faiths to respect and listen to a gospel that causes people to love their neighbors.

Biblical Principles:

1. James 1:27 says "Religion that God our Father accepts as pure and faultless is this: to look after orphans and widows in their distress and to keep oneself from being polluted by the world." *Our God is a God of compassion.* From the Old Testament commands to care for the poor, orphans, and widows, to the New Testament mandates, God commands and expects believers to care for the helpless. (Ruth 2:3)

2. *While compassion is a characteristic of the spirit-filled Christian* (Colossians 3:12, Philippians 2:1), *we need to be careful that we make decisions based on the Holy Spirit's leading and not our own emotions, which might be rooted in sinful desires for recognition or personal satisfaction* (Romans 8:5). If we are a living sacrifice (Romans 12:1) and trust in Him, He *will* direct our paths (Proverbs 3:5).

Chapter 10

Judas and God's Sovereignty

Friends

Not long after moving to the town that later became home to H.E.L.P.'s headquarters, we met a young couple who were starting a church. An American denomination had sponsored the Badals to go to seminary in India and continued to provide their salary and living expenses. They also had a supervising Indian pastor based in Kathmandu. According to Mr. Badal, he had suffered much for following Christ. As a high-caste Brahmin, he had lost his inheritance and family relationships after leaving Hinduism. His children and ours became fast friends, and we had a close and seemingly reciprocal friendship.

At the time, in 1998, we had prayed about whether or not to build a headquarters, and whether the land and building should be registered through an NGO. As foreigners, we were not allowed to purchase land or build a building. It must either be in the name of a Nepali, several Nepalis, an INGO, or an NGO. As a Hindu kingdom, we had heard from other expatriates that the existing government might discriminate against an NGO with Christian leaders and working with churches, though other colleagues suggested that we still pursue that route. Political chaos and continued danger to staff and volunteers in rural areas necessitated we must have an identifying agency, as well as formal registration to make sure we were above reproach legally and professionally. More difficulties arose in finding the correct person or

219

people to get signatures from for our registration as an NGO. At times no one really knew who was in charge of our district—the Nepali government, the Maoists, the police, or no one! As we encountered roadblocks to the creation of a registered in-country organization, we assumed this was simply because of all the government turmoil, or obstruction because of our Christian views. Later, however, we realized many of these blocks were actually constructed and deceitfully arranged by one of our own.

After asking God how we should proceed, a piece of land suitable for a H.E.L.P. headquarters became available at an excellent price. We knew that if we waited, our minimal funds would never be sufficient to purchase something; prices were sky-rocketing. Since we had made no progress in the NGO registration, Mr. Badal agreed to buy the land in his name temporarily. In fact, he promised, "It doesn't really matter, because this is God's land and I will never use it for myself and my family." He assisted Tim in designing the training center, finding a contractor, and managing the money for the building.[65] Over the next year, we began noticing costs were increasing, but as inflation was a reality and the nation's civil conflict increased costs, it did not seem exorbitant. We had complete trust in our friend and co-worker.

As H.E.L.P. grew and added more programs, God increased our fruit and the Badals continued to work with us in an indirect way. Our ministries in income generation and literacy blessed their small congregation, as well. Because Mr. Badal spent a majority of his time on the road, a H.E.L.P. donor offered to buy him a motorcycle. He built relations with other pastors, and his wife began more literacy classes in some of the nearby areas. During the next four years our friendship and united purpose with this family grew, and we continued

---

[65]   Until the arrival of Mr. Bajracharya in 2003, who took over administration and the building, literally saving H.E.L.P. financially.

working together as H.E.L.P. developed. Words cannot describe how much time we spent together, solidifying our friendship and trust with this couple. They were our closest and most trusted friends. On several occasions we met with Mr. Badal's denominational director in Kathmandu, who fully supported the couple's involvement in the community outreach of H.E.L.P., recognizing its important role in the growth of the church. In our minds, when we left Nepal, this couple would continue the work that God had begun. In addition, when we prayed about opening the children's home, they encouraged the idea and suggested a couple from their church to be the first house parents. They even assisted us in negotiating of a good price to rent first one floor, and later the entire building next to their own rented home and church for Jyoti Niwas.

In 2003, as we realized God was telling us that the time was approaching for us to transition more fully to indigenous leadership, and we mentioned this more and more to our Nepali team, we noted a slight change in the Badals. They became more demanding and controlling. Staff relations became strained. Mrs. Badal, in particular, began demanding things—control, money, honor. We assumed these were some transition issues. Prior to this shift in his relationship, we had offered Mr. Badal the position of national director of H.E.L.P. He had refused, saying he could not take the position due to his responsibilities at the church. Initially, we attributed this show of humility as integrity, but we later realized he refused the position as national director only because he anticipated stealing everything and dissolving H.E.L.P. and her sister NGO (which was in the process of being approved due to Mr. Bajracharya's efforts).

A New Vision for Jyoti Niwas

In one particularly noteworthy meeting, as our new training center, was being completed, our full-time staff insisted that they did *not* want the building for staff housing, but rather wanted the children in the newly opened Jyoti Niwas to move into the building. The building had a perimeter fence, good security, and surrounding fields for agriculture plots; by contrast, the current rented Jyoti Niwas facility was woefully inadequate. Mr. Bajracharya, our administrator, took the lead as he recognized the relational problems that were developing between the Badals and the rest of the H.E.L.P. team, though he was not sure of the cause. He wisely made changes to the final development of the building to accommodate the children—with dormitory space for girls and boys on different floors—rather than staff apartments, as originally designed. He added a second kitchen for the children. He also added a large kitchen below, with separate entrances and two floors for men and women, so those coming from distant regions for training at *Manthano* had living and training quarters. He foresaw that the large meeting room, which we had planned as a training and fellowship hall, could be used by the children when no trainees were present. Almost overnight, Mr. Bajracharya converted a building we had intended to use as staff housing and training center, to a combination of a children's home and a training center.

After this meeting and several following, Tim and I were shocked and hurt. We had designed the building and sacrificed not only our own finances, but also the finances of others. Yet our Nepali partners seemed so ungrateful! We agreed that the facility for Jyoti Niwas was too small, but this change in building plans would mean our staff would have to walk and ride the bus to the headquarters, and we would need an additional small office building on the premises. The children's home was not even in our original vision, and this change seemed to be limiting what *we saw* as God's direction.

In time, we recognized the wisdom of all of these decisions and the fact that the other staff were uncomfortable about the future because they distrusted the Badals. Several of our staff had heard them brag that *they* built the training center with *their* own money, and this was *their* work, not God's. Mr. Bajracharya, as well, had begun to distrust the couple, but did not want to wrongfully accuse them. In order to avoid a big conflict, he had suggested that it would be best to house the children of Jyoti Niwas in the building, to protect H.E.L.P's investment of land and property from this family. Though none of them directly communicated these concerns to us at this time, their direction averted later disaster. We misunderstood the hints but knew enough to trust our colleagues. In addition, we *did not* foresee how the children would use the same fields and animals to learn new farming and composting techniques alongside farmers coming from near and far to be trained in sustainable agriculture. More importantly, in our vision of discipleship, we failed to see how our committed full-time Christian staff would mentor and disciple the children as they grew, becoming an extended family and developing the teen vocational training program.

A Wolf in Sheep's Clothing

During the first six months after our departure from Nepal, God clarified the issues. Mr. Badal began to email us, claiming "my land, my property," and referring to *Manthano*, our newly completed training center as "belonging to me and my family." He demanded we relinquish everything to him; legally it *did* belong to him, according to Nepali law. Since we had not yet finished the paperwork for the NGO, the land was still in his name. We had later bought a second small adjoining piece of land in Mr. Bajracharya's name, in an attempt to protect H.E.L.P. from the very fate we were experiencing, however the piece of property with the building was in the Badals' name.

For months we corresponded by email (when it worked), hoping that our close friend and erring pastor would repent; instead, he persisted in his plan to seize H.E.L.P.'s property, including the farmer field training plots, animal husbandry areas, and new building which was now serving as Jyoti Niwas children's home and a training center for villagers all over the country. Our original literacy teacher and close friend, Mrs. Bajracharya, had recently accepted our offer to become H.E.L.P. national director. Leaving a lucrative position in the Middle East, she had a desire to serve her own people by sharing her faith and helping the poor. When she arrived back in Nepal in March 2004, issues with the Badals became very heated. She, too, hoped for reconciliation. God had other plans.

In April 2004, Tim returned for a visit, only a few months after we had left Nepal. While he was informally having tea with the mayor, chief political officer (chief district officer), and police chief, Mr. Bajracharya ran into the hotel with shocking news. "Badal is holding the literacy teacher training students hostage, as well as the children. He has hired some thugs and is demanding the keys and removal of everyone so he can take possession of what he claims is his land and property." The mayor looked at the police officer and said, "This is what we have been waiting for." They asked Tim to get in the car and drove down to the training center and orphanage, where a shocked Mr. Badal did not receive keys, but a ride to the jail. Interestingly, the police chief yelled at him, "You are Satan!" He voiced the feelings of the community against a man who claimed to follow Christ, but in reality was serving the enemy, and thwarting compassionate acts of kindness. Later, his wife was also jailed as his accomplice. The house parents who he had set up to be his allies also had to be dismissed, as they lied in court claiming that the Badal family had personally paid for the property. They had been told by him that they would share in the spoil.

As facts unfolded over time, the Badals' intentions and calculations amazed the entire team. Unbeknown to us, when this "wolf" realized we and the Nepalese staff would not willingly agree to transfer everything to his power, he had plotted to transfer H.E.L.P.'s land and training center to his father, a lawyer in town. Only one day prior to the land transfer, his father was walking to work at the city court and decided to ride the back of a tractor to save time. It was monsoon season and a landslide had blocked the road, so the driver instructed those riding on the back to disembark for safety. Senior Mr. Badal arrogantly refused, the trailer flipped, and he alone died.[66] God's judgment was sober, but Mr. Badal still did not repent. We approached his denominational director in Kathmandu, as well as the U.S.-based directors, none of whom recognized him as a wolf in sheep's clothing. Slowly, years of lies began unfolding. Though known as a pastor, he clearly had never followed Christ except in name. In addition, he was never disowned for his faith, nor suffered any of the injustices he claimed. He became a pastor as an easy way to make money, and an American denomination saw him as a promising young believer and paved his way. We and our national colleagues were deceived; he was finally showing his true colors. His sponsoring denomination never admitted their mistake and he is still an ordained minister.

Over the next five years, while the Holy Spirit was bringing people to Christ, uplifting the poor, and expanding our development programs, many of our staff and volunteers had to go from court

---

[66] One of the staff at the court shared this with us during the process of our court case.

case to court case, challenging the Badals rightful ownership of the land. He, of course, claimed that the money with which the land and building was purchased belonged to him, and that legally he had all rights. We had the burden of proof, and had not even completed the NGO process prior to this event, due to his efforts in blocking the transactions. In addition, our staff, particularly our dear brother and administrator Mr. Bajracharya, worked night and day to successfully complete the NGO application, making us a legal entity under a Nepali name. At case after case, hundreds of villagers from communities who had benefitted from H.E.L.P.'s ministry—both spiritually and physically—came forward to testify. "This is our center, our organization, and our children's home. This man did not give any money. This belongs to the people of our country." The local mayor, an ardent Hindu, was a dear friend of ours who believed in the work H.E.L.P. was doing for his community and the poor; he used his political influence in our favor. Lawyers, both Christian and non-Christian, worked with us to defend the right to keep the property and training center/orphanage for the people of Nepal rather than the devious individual claiming it.

Finally, the case went all the way to the supreme court of the country. We knew the history of this sort of problem well. We had heard of churches and other Christian organizations who had put the land and building in one or more local Christian's name, only to have them "backslide" and sell the land for profit. God once more proved his greatness and ultimate plan, and we won the case. As a landmark case, newspapers all over the country published our story, spreading the news of the work of H.E.L.P.'s sister NGO. In a way we never could have foreseen, the trials and court case proved that H.E.L.P. and her NGO were not just an organization, but rather a movement—a grassroots movement that could not be owned by a person, a church, or a denomination because it belonged to the people of the local communities and to the Lord.

Sadly, the Badals have not yet repented. Prior to the final Nepal Supreme Court decision, they resorted to criminal activities such as hiring an assassin to attempt to kill H.E.L.P.'s director, sending harassing messages, and even threatening to kidnap the children of our staff. The long ordeal was especially painful for all of our Nepali friends, because the one we had trusted and loved had become our "Judas." The couple served time in prison and even deceived some well-meaning Christians from another country who thought they were imprisoned for their faith, rather than for being criminals! Their children followed the parents and turned to crime. Those who had the opportunity to serve the Lord chose to serve money instead, and suffered the consequences.

Avoiding Wolves

The scripture frequently mentions that there are wolves in sheep's clothing among us. In 2 Timothy 4:10, Paul said, "Demas has forsaken us, having loved this present world." When we come from wealthy countries, presumably with money, we attract a type of people who are opportunists, or "rice Christians." Perhaps the most dangerous and common misdeed well-meaning Western Christians and churches commit is choosing young, promising new believers and sending them for Bible training as pastors. Even worse, instead of teaching them a vocational skill, these new pastors are paid by outside money, creating dependency, causing suspicion by locals, and resulting in the accusation that people are paid to be Christians (possibly an accurate assumption).

When we read about the early missions movement in Acts, we see no mention of people being paid for their ministry, except in specific cases of need and famine. Teaching pastors to be bi-vocational (having another job in addition to pastoring), and giving them skills to earn a living is a practical way for us to assist churches. Using theological education by extension, or locally based Bible trainings, allows for maturity within the home culture

> The apostle Paul made tents to support himself, and though he had led many people to the Lord, refrained from becoming financially dependent on others.

and avoids the stigma that "Christians are paid" or "they don't work, they just preach and foreigners pay them." All of these issues solidify suspicions that Christianity is a foreign religion motivated by imperialistic motives and encourages those who truly do not know Christ to pretend they do, for what they can gain. How different we should be!

Biblical Principles:

1. *Matthew 7:15 and Acts 20:29 tell us to expect wolves.* Often we are more susceptible as foreigners working in a different culture. God is sovereign and gracious. His plan to bring the good news to the nations (Revelation 14:6) cannot be thwarted, but we are wise to be careful in whom we trust and how we invest His resources.

2. As Paul writes in 1 Thessalonians 4:11-12, *our daily lifestyle should win the respect of the people around us because of our hard work and self-support.* The development, social, and economic work of H.E.L.P. gained us the respect of our neighbors of different faiths. Ambassadors for Christ must live the crucified life (Galatians 2:20) rather than luring others into a fake commitment for purposes of worldly gain. "For me to live is Christ and to die is gain." Phillipians 1:21

Chapter 11

Transitions and Sustainability

New Challenges for Sustainability

By March 2004, when Mrs. Bajracharya assumed leadership of H.E.L.P., things were far from running smoothly! The Badals had plunged us into a lengthy legal battle and the Ackerman family was experiencing financial difficulty and reverse culture shock back home in the United States. H.E.L.P.'s future did not look especially bright. In Nepal, the Maoist problem continued and inflation caused our ever-decreasing funds to dwindle further. We had nearly completed the *Manthano* training center, and the children had already moved in.

Back in the US, I was working eighty hours a week or more and bringing home almost no money because of my lack of medical business savvy and the unethical practices of some of my colleagues. Tim had been out of his field for too long, and changes in technology made it difficult for him to find a good job. As I was virtually living in the hospital or clinic, he could not search for other opportunities. The children did not adapt well to even a small Christian school, so Tim decided to stay home full-time to teach them, while also volunteering as the administrator for H.E.L.P., to allow our few resources and donations to be sent to Nepal. We dealt with problem after problem, wondering if the years were wasted or if God would grow the seeds we planted into something more.

Though communication was poor, with erratic electricity, poor phone connections, unreliable emails, and non-existent mail service, the Holy Spirit was working in and through our eighteen national Christian staff and hundreds of indigenous volunteers as they continued on in their labor of love, praying, working and teaching their friends and neighbors. Though they constantly requested our approval, all felt the freedom to develop their departments and programs based on God's leading, their training, and the experiences they had while working in villages and towns. When one method of teaching did not work, they tried another. When one community embraced new ideas, they tried the same approach in another community. Because of the great diversity of ethnic groups and languages within the country, our multi-lingual, multi-caste staff was able to help one another learn the best approach in various areas.

We continue to personally visit the H.E.L.P. team once or twice a year and communicate monthly with the director and periodically with the other staff. Limitations of communication media affect us, but we have constant spiritual and financial accountability, with lessening day-to-day accountability for specifics of ministry. Our full-time staff, literacy teachers, veterinary technicians, agriculturalists, and volunteer TBA, FCHW, VCHWs, and others all continue to serve as national missionaries to their own people. They too are constantly growing in their *love for the Lord their God* and their *love for their neighbor* as the wholistic gospel in the form of Christian community development continues to spread. By 2008, we had maps at the headquarters with pins showing where we were working or had worked, and prayer areas where many were still starving for the truth of Christ and for food and basic needs. We began to see that nearly all of the formerly unreached people groups within the Himalayas are now being reached, and our brothers and sisters strategically planned how to reach those who still had not heard of the Savior.

We see ourselves continuing to work with our national colleagues according to the New Testament apostles' example: preaching, teaching, and empowering local believers, then leaving them in charge and returning to encourage them regularly. In a poor country familiar with the temptation of all fallen human beings to be corrupted by money and power, we maintain strict accountability of funds and resources. As fellow Christians with the same Lord and same Holy Spirit, we recognize their ability to hear God's direction in leading His work, just as we do. In the past, we often saw God give us a vision for His work, and we imparted it to them. Now, it is more common that they have a vision *with* us, and sometimes even *before* we do, a sign of their spiritual maturity.

A recent example of this is in H.E.L.P.'s work in the terai area of Western Nepal, among the Tharu people and Dalits. Our burden was initially more focused on the spiritually needy Tibetan Buddhists of the Himalayas (a variety of castes), and the first ten years of development work encompassed many of these people groups. We later saw the great needs among the ex-Kamaiyas[67], as well as other high-risk, impoverished castes selling their daughters into prostitution. Though we had prayed and talked about these needs, our Nepali staff thought beyond us. Both Mr. Prajapati and the agriculture team, as well as Mr. Shrestha and the literacy team, recognized the root causes. They were approached by community leaders in these areas and despite suffering privation and hardships, they took literacy and income generation to these difficult-to-access communities. Mrs. Magar and the health team followed, improving maternal and child health in the area. The entire development team has seen a huge awakening among

---

[67] Kaimayas are a group of indentured servants who were officially freed by the Nepali government in 2000, but who practically are often enslaved to poverty and whose young daughters suffer the consequences.

people in this area for the gospel, and with the spiritual transformation and economic uplifting of the women and entire family, the risk of child prostitution is decreasing. Success comes slowly, but this simple approach of spiritual transformation coupled with economic alternatives proves dramatically more effective than more heroic rescue efforts to capture perpetrators or rescue girls at various border stations.

From 2004 to 2010, God's work through H.E.L.P. grew exponentially. Initially, due to the civil turmoil, strikes, closed roads, and danger from distant travel, we developed the Group Representative (GR) program. The multi-tiered level of accountability described in previous chapters was the only functional way we could meet the needs of communities in distant areas while maintaining the trainer-of-trainers model and providing follow-up in the field to learning activities. In 2009, the owner of land adjacent to our training center offered to sell his property for an excellent price. By keeping our administrative costs to nearly zero, we had saved what we thought would be enough money to build an additional separate training facility, allowing more space for our growing children, many of whom were older teens. Our national team agreed it was past time to separate the H.E.L.P. offices, training center, and fields from Jyoti Niwas, so we prayerfully began the process of building a second training center down the road.

Shortly after that decision was made, events at Jyoti Niwas clarified we must have a halfway house for our older boys, and more space for the children to fully manage their own fields and animals, both for sustainability of food for Jyoti Niwas, and in preparation for entering the workforce in a country with abysmal opportunities for employment. Mr. Bajracharya had tirelessly overseen construction of the initial center, but his health was rapidly deteriorating. His heart condition had worsened, and he was only able to walk short distances and work from home. Mr. Prajapati, Mr. Shah, and staff who were not out in the field conducting follow-up or training, stepped in to oversee the building project. Older boys in the orphanage provided much of the labor, learning bricklaying and painting. Prices skyrocketed and the cost exceeded our expectations, bringing all work to a halt.

By the end of 2010, we had no money, and our family had already exhausted our savings. We began to question God and wonder whether we had heard His direction or if we were outside of His will. We shared with our Nepali team, and all continued to do what they could to generate income by growing crops, raising animals, and cutting costs; they, too, were discouraged. On the one hand, we were seeing hundreds of churches planted, people coming to Christ in unreached areas and people groups, and thousands of farmers raised from starvation to fulfilled lives and adequate food. We witnessed communities transformed from dirt and disease to cleanliness and health, with protected water sources and toilets. We noted decreased orphans and fewer problems with prostitution in areas where the sustainable agriculture projects and health education took place. But even with all these wonderful changes, we had no marketers and no slick brochures or other means to let donors know what we were doing. In desperation we all prayed, night and day, and as God so often had done, he answered with just enough funding to care for every literacy class, farmer field school, staff member, and child. There were definitely no frills or extras, but over the next year we were able to complete the new training center and continue the existing programs.

In 2011, a new crisis came. From our inception in 1999, we had absolutely no staff turnover. Though we had added national (indigenous) missionaries who were professionals in their fields and trained them further, we had never had any (other than the Badals) leave. But Mr. Shah, the CMA I had trained and watched mature as a Christian with excellent public health and diagnostic skills, and his wife, Miss Tamang, whom he had met while they were both working for H.E.L.P., decided they wanted to pursue further Bible training and seminary in India. Mr. Raju, the young man we had educated as a veterinary technician, decided to go with them. Though we knew all three would later return to serve Christ and their country in their bi-vocational fields, it was a time of great transition for H.E.L.P. In addition, Mr. Bajracharya, our accountant, friend, and administrator of amazing talents, left us to be with the Lord. This left Mrs. Bajracharya, our dear friend and H.E.L.P.'s in-country director, a widow with two teenage daughters—alone and exhausted after months of constant caring for him.

God always does provide, though. He brought another mature Christian, Mr. Sangam, with even further experience in poultry to join the animal husbandry department. He then brought one of our GRs of ten years to be our Jyoti Niwas director, to both mentor our children and lead our vocational training. As we searched for other qualified staff, the Lord provided scholarships through generous donors for four of the orphanage boys to go to school for further education as well as be part-time H.E.L.P. junior staff in agriculture, animal husbandry, and health departments. After completion of their degrees, they will first be mentored by, and eventually work alongside other staff, replacing the three who left.

As we pray and strategize with the team, I frequently have asked: "If we have the money, do we need another full-time staff to oversee the literacy classes or another staff to oversee and develop the agriculture trainings?" Where our ideas are frequently to expand the number of staff or programs, our team often advises differently. "Let's utilize our GRs and train them further. Let them train and supervise those in the district." They recognize the limitations of funds and resources, and think of practical ways to stretch them further. They also recognize that to empower communities, we need more local people working and supervising the development. As usual, our reliance on them for direction has resulted in a more effective and long-lasting development.

The Need for a Wholistic Approach

In our lifelong journey to effectively take the good news and to disciple those who have not heard of Christ *while we love the Lord and love our neighbors* by teaching them to provide for their physical and spiritual needs, we believe the Lord is encouraging those in development work and missions to recognize the need for a wholistic approach. The Apostle Paul prayed for young believers who, like young believers in the Himalayas, had recently left idolatry:

> *May God himself, the God of peace, sanctify you through and through. May your whole spirit, soul and body be kept blameless at the coming of our Lord Jesus Christ.* 1 Thessalonians 5:23

Followers of Christ must be wholistic in their approach, looking for causes of spiritual and physical deprivation, and seeking to address the root issues. Virtually every

> **Christian community developers must minister to the body, soul, and spirit, or the work is destined for failure.**

miracle in the gospels precedes or follows teaching about the kingdom of God. Our Savior ministered to the poor and sick, but He brought healing and relief from physical needs *with* preaching the kingdom of God. In the same way, we as His disciples must not separate human physical needs from spiritual needs, and we must not exclude either from our ministry.

> *"Hearing that Jesus had silenced the Sadducees, the Pharisees got together. One of them, an expert in the law, tested him with this question: "Teacher, which is the greatest commandment in the Law?"*

> *Jesus replied: "Love the Lord your God with all your heart and with all your mind." This is the first and greatest commandment. And the second is like it: "Love your neighbor as yourself."*
> Matthew 22:37-39

As ambassadors for Christ—His hands and His feet—we must look to these two greatest commandments that our Lord gave. Sustainable Christian community development is a spiritual movement, which develops communities not only in the physical sense, but also in the spiritual sense.

> *"For our struggle is not against flesh and blood, but against the rulers, against the authorities, against the powers of this dark world . . ."* Ephesians 6:12

We must disciple and train national believers to love the Lord first, and then to demonstrate that love to their neighbors. In Christian community development, we spiritually disciple and encourage people, while at the same time *empowering believers* through non-formal education (literacy), agriculture and animal husbandry skills, health improvement, economic development, and compassionate ministries to orphans and the helpless. The believers, then, demonstrate practical love to their neighbors as they teach their own community these same skills, with the passion and commitment that comes only through a personal walk with Jesus Christ.

We pray that through this story, mission leaders, individuals, and churches will be challenged to revisit *how* we are to evangelize, plant churches, and disciple. Our current western trends of short-term missions, high-dollar projects, and quick-fix methods simply do not line up with the example of Jesus, Paul, and the apostles. It is time for the church to awaken and recognize that if we want to be a part of the great work to bring all nations and ethnos to Christ's throne as a perfect bride, and to bring about (with the Holy Spirit's power) mature, indigenous, self-sustaining churches, we cannot continue with our current methods.

For those who seek a more wholistic way to plant sustainable, mature national churches that are not dependent on foreign funds and leadership, we hope this story will be an encouragement and inspiration. To those who want no glory for themselves or their church, but want the glory to go to God, this is an effective scriptural approach to disciple the nations. We pray the work God has allowed us to begin will continue to grow and spread, until every man, woman, and child in the Himalayan mountains of Asia will know the true Creator, and have an opportunity to understand Him in their own culture, with a gospel unadulterated by the western world. We also pray that believers in Christ will recognize Christian community development as the most Biblically based means of both partnering with and empowering nationals to develop their own communities, plant their own churches, and minister to the body, soul, and spirit.

To God be the Glory, Great Things He Has Done!

For more information on Health Environmental and Learning Program, visit www.missionforhelp.org or email admin@mission forhelp.org.

All proceeds from the sale of this book are donated to Health Environmental and Learning Program.

Questions for Group and Individual Study

Chapter 1

1. Discuss what Romans 10:14-15 says about those who bring good news. Historically, have Christian missionaries always been "beautiful feet" to the people they came to live among? Discuss good and bad examples.

2. Do those who have not heard the gospel have any witness of a Creator God? If so, do we really need to go to them at all? (See Ecclesiastes 3:11, Romans 1:19-20.)

3. Should outside agencies or churches support mission outreaches in areas of the world with established churches and many national Christians? Should the prophecy of Matthew 24:14 and promise of Revelation 5:9 affect how we spend our time and resources?

4. Review *Operation World* (available at www.ivpress.com/operationworld) and recent statistics available on the spiritual conditions in the Himalayas (India, Nepal, Bhutan, Pakistan, China). What do you know about the beliefs of Tibetan Buddhists and Hindus?

Chapter 2

1. Consider Philippians 2:7-8. Do you think most mission work today is incarnational? Does this affect the impact on a country or people group?

2. Do you think our American "fast food" mentality of trying to minister to people without studying their language and culture affects our mission outreaches? Do short-term mission trips

allow for incarnational missions? Can mission compounds (particularly hospitals on compounds) still be effective? If so, how? Study Acts 13-28, and compare Paul's methods of missions to efforts of churches today—either short or long-term.

3. Is it acceptable for American missionaries to live at a higher standard of living than those they minister to, especially in the developing world? Does this hinder their witness? Do you see this example in Jesus' life or among the early Christians and missionaries? (See Matthew 8:20, Acts 2:42-47, Philippians 4:10-19.)

4. Should those with young children go to remote or physically dangerous areas of the world? What does Jesus mean in Luke 14:28-33 when he says we should "count the cost"?

Chaptler 3

1. How can we know if spiritual leaders in the church are properly guiding those on the field? Read about some of the conflicts between leadership in the church and servants of Christ on the field who dramatically impacted the world. How did some of those seemingly not submissive to spiritual authority actually demonstrate submission to their true authority, God? (Examples: Martin Luther, William Carey, Amy Carmichael, Mary Slessor, Gladys Aylward.) In which situations is it biblically correct for church/mission agency leadership to reprimand or stop fellowship with those in positions of spiritual leadership on a foreign field, or even at home? (See Matthew 18:15-17.)

2. Discuss the scripture references in the chapter. How does Romans 8:28 relate to Romans 8:29? How do you see God working to create you into His workmanship, so He can use

you more? Have you experienced the kind of joy described Psalm 126:6?

3. When we pray the Lord's prayer "your kingdom come, your will be done, on earth as it is in heaven," what are we really praying? Is that what we really want? (See Matthew 6:10.)

4. Have there been times in your life when people caused you harm, like Joseph's brothers did, but God used it for His glory? Review Genesis 50:20 and the story of Joseph. Discuss this, and how you were able to forgive those who sinned against you (or want to be able to do so).

Chapter 4

1. Read Phillipians 2: 1-18. Do those serving in missions or even in Christian development work seek to glorify the Lord, or themselves? How about churches, organizations, or missions? How can we individually and corporately have the "mind" or attitude of Christ as in Philippians 2? Do you? Do your church or agency outreaches? What can we in the church do to encourage an attitude of true humility in service?

2. Read Romans 12:1,2. What is the relationship between being a living sacrifice and having an attitude of humility? How do these attitudes relate to the promises of Proverbs 3:4,5 and Proverbs 16:3?

3. Read Acts 27 and 28. Do you think Paul anticipated the opportunities he had on the island of Malta when he was suffering in the shipwreck? How should we react to changes in our plans or clarification of vision God gives us as we are serving Him?

4. How deep are the relationships which Paul develops as he shares the gospel? (Acts 20:36-38, I Corinthians 1:4, Galatians

4:12-14). What sort of relationships should we seek to develop with those we share our lives with?

Chapter 5

1. Do you agree or disagree that loving the Lord must be first, before loving your neighbor, for effective Christian community development? (See Matthew 22:37-39.)

2. Look up the word *poor* in a Bible concordance. Who are the poor? What is the Christian's responsibility toward the poor? How do you see the poor cared for in the Old Testament? (See Leviticus 19:10 and Ruth 2:7.) Do you see this in the New Testament? (See Galatians 2:10, Acts 4:34, and Acts 9:36.) Do you think Christian community development is a scriptural means to care for the poor and lead people to Christ?

3. Do you agree or disagree with the following statement: "Meeting physical needs is more than building a hospital or sending short-term medical mission teams. Health and social needs must be addressed at the community level over a long period of time." What is the scriptural basis for your position?

4. Should Christian mission outreaches focus on spiritual needs, physical needs, or both? Read and discuss Matthew 14:14-20, James 2:18-20, Luke 9:25.

5. Based on II Thessalonians 3:10, would the Apostle Paul support handouts of free food and clothing on a regular basis to those who do not work? How can the church respond compassionately to the welfare mentality of our society and world?

Chapter 6

1. In assessing community programs and in church planting, many leaders advocate national leadership and partnership, but often this may be in word, rather than in action. In many areas, leadership has already been determined by existing social structures. In Hindu and Buddhist societies, for example, caste dictates relations. Even in church hierarchy, the higher caste church member may become a pastor, as he is the most educated, or has already been in a leadership role. How can those in missions develop true national leadership, rather than a partnership in name only? How can applying the principals of discipleship and 2 Timothy 2:2 guide us?

2. Many Christian and non-Christian agencies target social needs such as prostitution, child labor, and other heartbreaking problems. Which do you think is a more effective, sustainable way to stop these social ills: to focus on the problem or to prevent it through sustainable Christian community development? Why do you think most organizations and people prefer the more dramatic rescues or problem-focused approach? Which approach is more financially sustainable? Which approach lends itself to the discipleship principles above?

3. Discuss administrative avenues through which followers of Christ can address the needs of the poor in a Biblical way. What do you see as the pros and cons of INGOs, NGOs, non-profit organizations, denominations, and purely secular organizations? Investigate some organizations you have heard of or to which you personally contribute and see what portion of their budget goes to overhead costs—staff salaries, administrative costs, etc.

4. Have you witnessed effective or ineffective use of the discipleship principles in missions outreach? Does this teaching that Paul refers to in 2 Timothy 2:2 mean only spiritual teaching? Could it refer to training in areas of health, agriculture, or veterinary work? How quickly can we disciple another?

Chapter 7

1. Why is it so important that any effort in Christian community development draw strength and direction from the True Vine? Read John 15:5-15 and discuss.

2. How does the unity—or disunity—of various churches and mission organizations, or even the duplicated efforts of secular development agencies, affect the success of community development? What can be done to change this?

3. In Romans 12:4-5 the Apostle Paul discusses the members of the body and the different roles we each have based on the gifts God has given us. How does this relate to developing a team and mobilizing people to help their community?

Chapter 8

1. Review the passage I John 3:16-24. What is the relationship between obedience to God, love, and our actions. How does Christian community development, as described in this chapter, reflect a biblical example of how the church should function?

2. Discuss the concept of "reports" for success required for most development agencies and often by mission boards or churches. Though the scripture clearly indicates there is needed accountability, what kind of accountability do you think we encourage by requiring certain types of data? How can that be changed?

Chapter 9

1. Do you think we should send funds to sponsor children in other countries? Why or why not? How do we know the money is received by those children or utilized wisely?

2. In our churches, do we primarily look to other sources (government agencies, secular non-profits) to help the needy? Should we? How can we change this?

3. Can we hurt people by giving them help, even if they are vulnerable and needy? How can we obey Christ's mandate to care for orphans and widows without hurting them by enabling laziness or robbing local believers of their opportunity to be blessed by helping those in need?

4. Do you think orphanages can be a way for individuals in poverty-stricken areas to exploit donors or agencies? How do we know if the children living in these homes really don't have families to care for them since there are innumerable examples of families who lie and hire agents to get their children into homes, as well as crafty individuals who put their own children and relatives into homes for support? Should US churches start orphanages and expensive institutions that local Christians cannot continue to support in the future?

5. Many church teams make short-term trips to developing nations (often 1-4 weeks) to minister to orphans. How do you think this could affect national Christians' ministry of those in charge of the orphanage? How does it affect the children emotionally to have people come and go? Is it a wise use of God's resources?

Chapter 10

1. We often claim to work in partnership with local/national churches or believers. Do financial interests such as paying the pastors, building the buildings, or bringing teams from the United States to assist in construction or help in major operations run the risk of corrupting individuals or the body of believers? Read 1 Thessalonians 4:11-12. How do you think this relates to how we partner with others in poor communities?

2. Is there an example in Scripture of people being paid for doing God's work of preaching, teaching, and evangelism? Consider 1 Timothy 5:18, which says that "a workman is worthy of his hire." Is this referring to basic needs, or a comfortable salary?

3. How will these principles affect how we train young leaders abroad or even in the United States? Can bi-vocational training prevent some of this dependency?

4. How can Western Christians be an example in this area? By providing full support for those preaching, teaching, doing evangelism, and church planting, could we be presenting a poor example? How can we set a better example?

5. In our attempt to "nationalize" our ministries, do we quickly support evangelists from other countries, rather than ensuring nationally run organizations are not get-rich-quick schemes for "rice Christians"? (those who pretend to believe to gain material benefit such as rice, but who have no true faith in Christ) What should we do if someone from another country requests support to preach or evangelize as a national missionary?

Chapter 11

1. How do you think it might impact believers in developing countries to see a missionary without any obvious means of income? (For example, only preaching or teaching, with no other skills.) Could this affect those who come to Christ and their understanding of the job of a church leader?

2. Do you think our short-term mission trips are more evangel-tourism, or true missionary journeys? How does a modern mission trip compare to the missionary journeys of Acts? What benefits or harms could such a trip cause?

3. Notice the context of Acts 21:35. Begin reading in Acts 21:32. Why do you think the Apostle Paul emphasized to the Ephesians that he supplied his own personal needs and those of his companions, and yet reminds them that it is more blessed to give than receive?

4. Read and discuss Matthew 22:27-29. What happens if we put the second commandment before the first? How could that lead to pride or burn out?

5. Discuss the methods used by Health Environmental Learning Program to meet physical needs and bring the gospel to those who have not heard of Christ. Do you think these methods are in agreement with the scripture?

6. What do you, your family, or your church plan to do after reading this book and contemplating the scriptures mentioned. Review Matthew 25:31-46. How do you or your church need to change your mission focus—where you send people or money? Are you focusing on only physical or only spiritual needs?

7. Read Matthew 24:4-14. If we change our approach to a more biblical Great Commission, one which is wholistic as Jesus's ministry and that of the apostles, loving God first and loving our neighbor, can we hasten the coming of Christ (verse 14)?

About the Author

Dr. Lani K. Ackerman is a family physician, associate professor of family medicine, wife, and mother of four children. Her publications include articles in many peer-reviewed journals and textbook chapters. She lectures and teaches internationally on many family medicine, global, preventive health, and missions topics. She has spent nearly half of her career in international development work, and most of her 25 years of practice after residency, both in patient care and in education of medical students and residents. Lani, a graduate of Texas A&M University and College of Medicine, and her husband, Tim, and family claim Texas as their US home. They are the founders of, and currently serve as the volunteer CEOs of Health Environmental and Learning Program (H.E.L.P.) In addition to a full-time job in clinical practice and as associate director of academics at a family medicine residency program, Lani enjoys spending time with her family in church and community work with refugees and internationals, serving in music ministries, and mentoring resident physicians.